new business card graphics

P•I•E Books

new business card graphics

First published in Japan 1996 by **P·I·E BOOKS**
#301 4-14-6, Komagome Toshima-ku, Tokyo 170 Japan
TEL: 03-3949-5010 FAX: 03-3949-5650
ISBN4-89444-004-0 C3070P16000E

First published in Germany 1996
by **NIPPAN** Nippon Shuppan Hanbai Deutschland GmbH
Krefelder Str. 85, D-4000 Dusseldorf 11 (Heerdt), Germany
TEL: 0211-5048089 FAX: 0211-5049326
ISBN3-910052-82-7

Printed in Japan

Credit Format

Client/Country/Type of business

CD: Creative director

AD: Art director

D: Designer

CW: Copywriter

I: Illustrator

GD: Graphic designer

DF: Design firm

CONTENTS

序文

名刺：
小型で厚めの紙に、
名前・住所・所属先などの情報を印刷した物。

日頃何気なく目にしている名刺も、少し見方を変えると全く違った面が見えてくるものです。ビジネスの視点でみると、単なる"情報"でしかない名刺が、ほんの少しデザイン に目を向けただけで、明るく元気なもの、シンプルで洗練されたもの、ポップで楽しいもの、シックでおしゃれなものとさまざまな表情をみせてくれます。今回、ここに 収録された世界各地からの約９００作品をご覧になれば、その表情の多さに皆さんもきっと驚かれることでしょう。名刺も個性を表現するための一手段 あるとすればそれも頷けることです。
さて、今回本書を編集するにあたって感じたことといえば、以前ではクリエイター関係の業種に偏りがちだったデザイン性の高い

作品がサービス業や製造業などにも見られるようになったこと、
スノーボードメーカーをはじめ各メーカー、クリエイターの今
までにない積極的かつ斬新なデザインスタイルが加わったことな
どです。経費削減が謳われていますが、デザインにはますますみ
がきがかかるばかりのようです。
今回は、以前ではあまり見ることのできなかったロシア、旧ユー
ゴスラビア、スロベニアなど東ヨーロッパからの参加もあり、
世界各国から力作が勢ぞろいしました。
皆さんはどんな視点で御覧になりますか？
最後に、本書のために貴重な作品をお送り下さいました皆様、
ならびに制作に当たりご協力頂きました皆様に心よりお礼を申し
上げます。

ピエ・ブックス編集部

Business card:
a small card printed
with information
that usually includes the bearer's name, address and place of employment or affiliation.

So frequently are we obliged to glance at business cards in the course of our daily lives that most people rarely give them a second thought. But if we stop to examine them a little more carefully we come to see them in an entirely new light. From a strictly business standpoint, cards are nothing more than the information they convey. There is little scope for variation until we consider their design. Only then do we notice a surprisingly wide range of different types. There are bright, cheery cards, and simple, tasteful ones. Some set out to be hip or amusing while others are more stylish.

Well designed cards tended at one time to be specifically associated with business in creative fields, but they are now to be found in all business areas, and particularly in the industrial and service sectors. We also find brand new businesses such as snowboard manufacturers coming up with a completely fresh look. Considering that the need to cut costs is a priority everywhere these days, the design and quality of business cards is of a remarkably high standard.

Part of the explanation is of course that in business, one's card helps to make a favorable impression at that all-important first meeting. But people also seem to have realized that the cards they pass out say something significant about their individual personalities.

This time we have included card designs from various eastern European countries such as Russia, the former Yugoslavia and Slovenia, which have rarely been available before, and so this edition is a more truly representative selection of top-class business cards from around the world. We hope that after looking through it, you'll be encouraged to take a better look at the business cards that come your way.

We at PIE Books would like to take this opportunity to express our thanks to the many people who have contributed to this volume.

P·I·E BOOKS

Visitenkarten:
kleine Karten,
bedruckt mit Informationen,
die in der Regel den Namen des Inhabers, seine Adresse
und seine Firma oder Gesellschaft beinhalten.

In unserem Alltag sind wir so oft gehalten, auf Visitenkarten zu
schauen, daß die meisten Leute selten einen weiteren Gedanken
daraufverschwenden. Aber wenn wir innehalten, um sie etwas
genauer zu examinieren, kann es passieren, daß wir sie in einem
völlig neuem Licht sehen. Aus dem reinen Geschäftsaspekt
heraus sind die Visitenkarten nichts mehr als die Information, die
sie beinhalten. Es gibt wenig Raum für Variationen, bis wir ihr
Design in Betracht ziehen. Erst dann erkennen wir die
überraschend große Vielfalt. Da gibt es glanzvolle, laute Karten
und es gibt einfache, geschmackvolle. Andere sind modisch oder
amüsant, während weitere besonders stilvoll anmuten.

Gut gestaltete Karten wurden bis vor einiger Zeit besonders
Firmen im Kreativbereich zugeordnet. Heute jedoch kann man
perfektes Design in allen Geschäftsbereichen finden,
insbesondere auch in der Industrie und im Dienstleistungssektor.
Auch kommen brandneue Firmen auf den Markt, wie etwa
Snowboard-Hersteller, die mit einem völlig neuen, frischen Look

auftreten. Bedenkt man, daß die Kosten heutzutage überall Priorität genießen, dann sind das Design und die Qualität der Visitenkarten von einem bemerkenswert hohen Standard.

Eine Erklärung ist natürlich, daß im Geschäftsleben die Visitenkarte hilft, bei dem höchstwichtigen ersten Meeting einen günstigen Eindruck zu vermitteln. Auch haben anscheinend die Leute realisiert, daß die Visitenkarten, die sie ausgeben, etwas wichtiges über ihre individuelle Persönlichkeit aussagen. Erstmals können wir in diesem Buch bisher kaum verfügbare Visitenkartendesigns aus verschiedenen osteuropäischen Staaten wie Russland, Yugoslawien und Slowenien zeigen. So beinhaltet diese Ausgabe eine noch bessere repräsentative Sammlung von erstklassigen Visitenkarten aus aller Welt. Wir hoffen, daß, nachdem Sie dieses Buch in Ruhe betrachtet haben, Sie in Zukunft einen noch kritischeren Blick auf die Visitenkarten werfen, die Ihnen vorgelegt werden.

Wir von P·I·E Books möchten uns hiermit bei allen, die zu diesem Buch beiget ragen haben, recht herzlich bedanken.
P·I·E Books

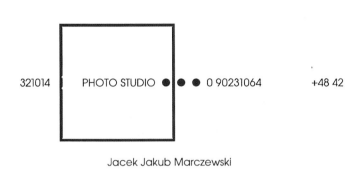

321014 PHOTO STUDIO ● ● ● 0 90231064 +48 42

Jacek Jakub Marczewski

Nataša Šarić
Kreator 013 520 901

OPPOSITE PAGE: **STUDIO VRZESIEŃ** (Poland) Design デザイン CD, AD, D: Tadeusz Piechura CW: Andrzej Wrzesień DF: Atelier Tadeusz Piechura

1. **JACEK JAKUB MARCZEWSKI** (Poland) Photographer 写真家 CD, AD, D, CW: Tadeusz Piechura DF: Atelier Tadeusz Piechura

2. **NATAŠA ŠARIĆ** (Yugoslavia) Fashion designer ファッション デザイナー CD, AD, D, I: Slavimir Stojanović DF: SMS Bates Saatchi & Saatchi Advertising Balkans

3. **FLAMINGO STUDIO INC.** (Japan) Graphic design グラフィック デザイン D: Billy Blackmon DF: Flamingo Studio Inc.

4. **BORIS MILJKOVIĆ** (Yugoslavia) Designer デザイナー CD, AD, D, I: Slavimir Stojanović DF: SMS Bates Saatchi & Saatchi Advertising Balkans

5. **JAAP STAHLIE** (Netherlands) Photographer 写真家 CD, AD, D: Jacques Koeweiden / Paul Postma DF: Koeweiden Postma Associates

1 2
3
4 5

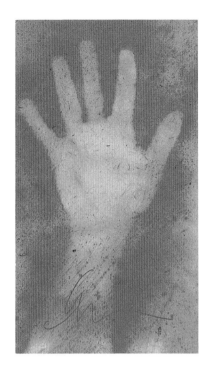

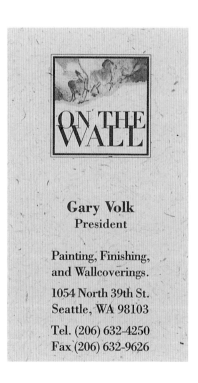

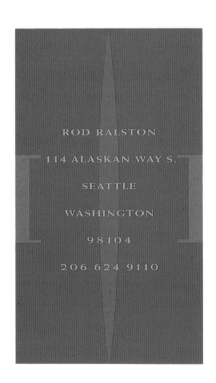

1. **BRADBURY DESIGN INC.** （Canada） Design **デザイン** AD, D: Catharine Bradbury DF: Bradbury Design Inc.

2. **ON THE WALL** （USA） Painter **ペインター** CD, AD, D: Rick Eiber I: Cave Dweller DF: Rick Eiber Design

3. **ROD RALSTON** （USA） Photographer **写真家** AD, D: Jack Anderson D: Julie Keenan / Mary Chin Hutchison DF: Hornall Anderson Design Works, Inc.

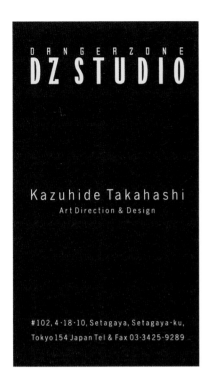

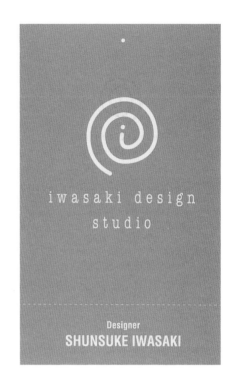

1. **DZ STUDIO** （Japan） Graphic design　グラフィック デザイン　AD, D, T: Kazuhide Takahashi　DF: DZ Studio

2. **PARADOX INC.** （Japan） Graphic design　グラフィック デザイン　D: Katsunori Tajima　DF: Paradox Inc.

3. **IWASAKI DESIGN STUDIO** （Japan） Graphic design　グラフィック デザイン　AD, D: Shunsuke Iwasaki　DF: Iwasaki Design Studio

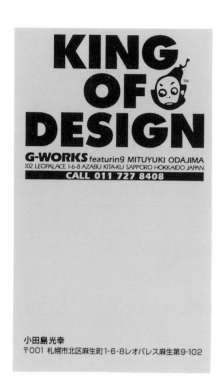

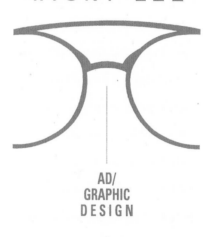

1. **G-WORKS** （Japan） Advertising design 広告デザイン AD, D: Mitsuyuki Odajima DF: G-Works

2. **KATHY CALDERWOOD** （USA） Design デザイン AD, D, I: Chalkley Calderwood DF: Paul Davis Studio

3. **MILOŠ SOLDATOVIĆ** （Yugoslavia） Photographer 写真家 CD, AD, D, I: Slavimir Stojanović DF: SMS Bates Saatchi & Saatchi Advertising Balkans

4. **SUZANNE CRAIG** （USA） Artist アーティスト CD, AD, D: Sonia Greteman DF: Greteman Group

5. **WICKY'S GRAPHICS** （USA） Graphic design グラフィック デザイン CD, AD, D, I: Wicky W. Lee DF: Wicky's Graphics

6. **PLUS-ONE** （Japan） Package design パッケージ デザイン CD, AD, D, DF: Plus-one

1 2 3

4 5 6

9911 West Pico Blvd
11th Floor
Los Angeles
CA 90035 USA
Tel: 0101 310 772 7485
Fax: 0101 310 772 7487
mobile: 0378 523606

1 **REED INFORMATION SERVICES** （UK） Publisher 出版 CD, AD: Andy Ewan D: Anne Kristen Nybo P, I: Emma Parker DF: Design Narrative

1. **TONY DELGADILLO DESIGN** （USA） Design デザイン AD, D: Tony Delgadillo DF: Tony Delgadillo Design

2. **KOWALSKI DESIGNWORKS** （USA） Graphic design グラフィック デザイン CD: Stephen Kowalski
AD, D: Janèl Apple D: Vanessa Wyers P: George Post DF: Kowalski Designworks, Inc.

1

2

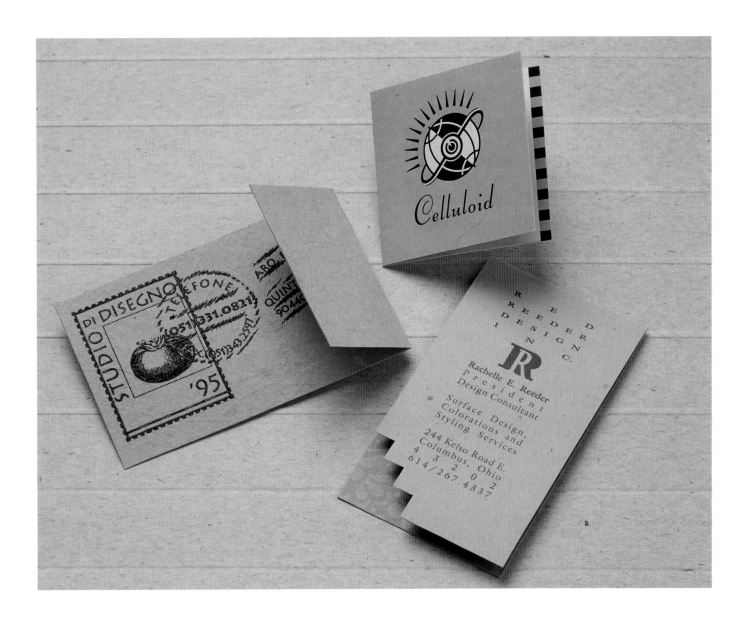

1. **CELLULOID STUDIOS** （USA）Animation studio　アニメーション スタジオ　D, I: Mark Fox　DF: BlackDog

2. **STUDIO DI DISEGNO** （Brazil）Graphic design　グラフィック デザイン　AD, D: Renata Rizzo Silveira　DF: Studio DI Disegno

3. **RED REEDER DESIGN INC.** （USA）Fabric design　ファブリック デザイン
CD: Rachelle E. Reeder　AD: Eric Rickabaugh　D: Tina Zientarski　DF: Rickabaugh Graphics

4. **CAMERAD, INC.** （USA）Photography　写真　CD, AD, D: Charles Shields　DF: Shields Design

5. **THE COOK EDITIONS, LTD.** （USA）Publisher　出版　CD, AD, D: Steve Rousso　DF: Rousso + Associates

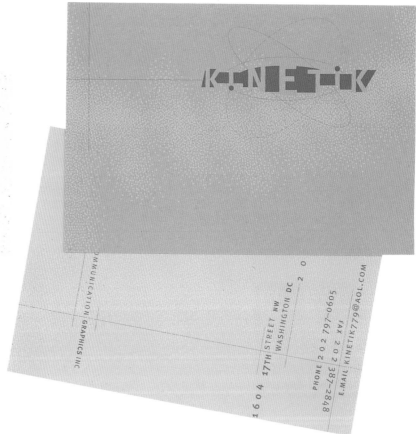

1. **ADÈLE NAUDÉ SANTOS AND ASSOCIATES** （USA） Architecture 建築設計 D: Kerry Polite DF: Polite Design

2. **ALEXANDRE JANVIER** （Germany） Designer デザイナー D: Alexandre Janvier

3. **ROBIN HASSETT PHOTOGRAPHY** （USA） Photography 写真 CD, AD, D, I: Charles Shields DF: Shields Design

4. **DOGMA** （Portugal） Design デザイン CD, AD, D: Emanuel Barbosa DF: Emanuel Barbosa Design

5. **KINETIK COMMUNICATION GRAPHICS, INC.** （USA） Graphic design グラフィック デザイン
AD: Samuel G. Shelton AD, D: Jeffrey S. Fabian D: Mimi Massé / Amy Gustincic DF: Kinetik Communication Graphics, Inc.

IDENTITY CRISIS?

HOTLINE 408.354.6726

sonny williams productions inc.

887 west marietta st nw
studio m-209
atlanta georgia · 30318

tel 404.892.5551
fax 404.892.8131

typo
technic
heinz

Erika Heinz

t·t

Typografik und

Desktop-Publishing mit

Lasertechnologie

Forststraße 58 a

A-6890 Lustenau

T 05577/84505

F 05577/84505-15

typo
technic
heinz

t·t

1. **THARP DID IT** (USA) Graphic design グラフィック デザイン D, CW: Rick Tharp DF: Tharp Did It

2. **SONNY WILLIAMS PHOTOGRAPHY** (USA) Photography 写真 CD: Mike Melia D: Todd Brooks DF: Melia Design Group

3. **TYPO TECHNIC HEINZ** (Austria) Typographer タイポグラファー CD, AD, D: Sigi Ramoser D: Stefan Gassner

Ted Heller
Editor
tel: 212-258-7410
fax: 212-258-7440

Nickelodeon Magazine
1515 Broadway
New York, NY 10036

Anthony Nex Photography
8749 West Washington Boulevard
Culver City California 90232
tel 310.836.4357 fax 310.837.2646

1. **NICKELODEON** （USA） Publisher 出版 CD, AD, D: Laurie Kelliher I: Michael Bartalos DF: World Egg
2. **ANTHONY NEX PHOTOGRAPHY** （USA） Photography 写真 CD, AD: Stan Evenson D: Angie Boothroyd DF: Evenson Design Group
3. **ART STUFF** （USA） Design デザイン CD, AD, D: Ellie Leacock DF: Art Stuff

1 2 3 4 5 **6**

6

the sixth sense productions

evélyn teplova

director of design

222 west 14th street
suite 3d
new york, ny 10011
718.935.1923
212.633.8958

SHINSUKE MOCHIDA
SINDBAD DESIGN
Daikanyama-Tokyū-Apartment #405, 20-23, Daikanyama-chō
Shibuya-ku, Tokyo150 / Tel.03.3461.4088 / Fax.03.3461.4486
Art Director

Art Director

持 田 慎 介

SINDBAD DESIGN
0334614088

Michael Furman Photographer

Telephone
215. 925. 4233
Facsimile
215. 925. 6108

115 Arch Street
Philadelphia,
Pennsylvania
19106

Michael Furman

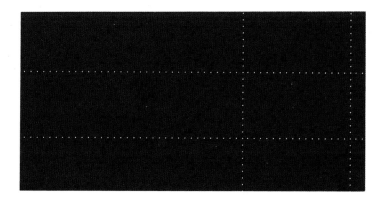

1. **6TH SENSE PRODUCTIONS** （USA）Design **デザイン** CD, AD, D: Evelyn Teploff D: Suzie Chu
2. **SINDBAD DESIGN** （Japan）Graphic design **グラフィック デザイン** AD, D: Shinsuke Mochida DF: Sindbad Design
3. **MICHAEL FURMAN** （USA）Photographer **写真家** D: Kerry Polite DF: Polite Design

1
2
3

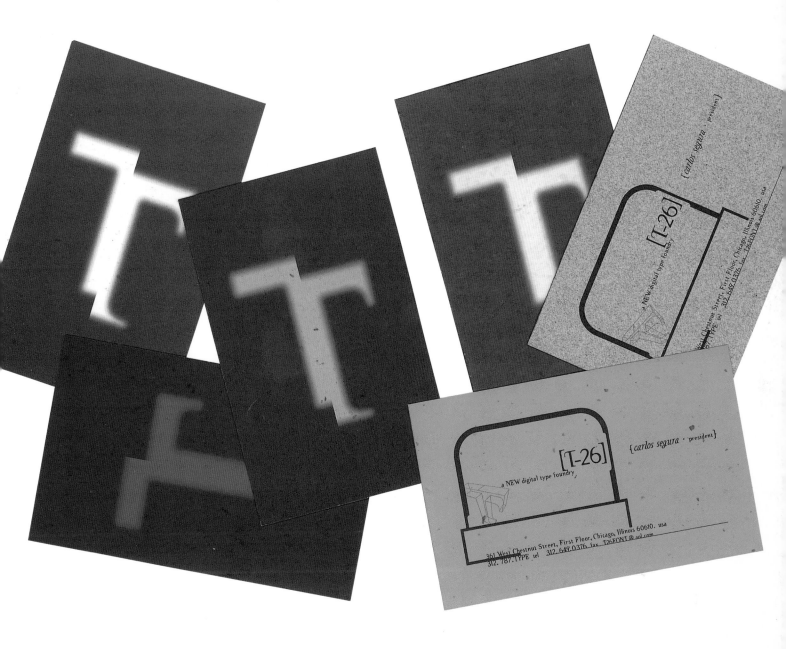

OPPOSITE PAGE: **BLEU ÉLASTIQUE** （France）Graphic design グラフィック デザイン　CD, AD, D: Pascal Béjean　DF: Bleu Élastique

1. **[T-26] DIGITAL TYPE FOUNDRY** （USA）Printing 印刷　CD, AD, D: Carlos Segura　DF: Segura Inc.

2. **HON SOO TIEN** （USA）Designer デザイナー　CD, AD, D: Hon Soo Tien　P: Charlie Lim Photography Studio

1

2

rich
ards
hiro

3 7 V A L L E Y **C I R C L E** M I L L V A L L E Y **C A** 9 4 9 4 1 **T E L / F A X** 4 1 5 3 8 0 **8** 8 2 3

jonathan woolf
ba hons dip arch riba

w o o l f a r c h i t e c t s

49-51 rathbone street   t 071 637 0991   f 071 637 0344
london w1p 1an

S P A N G E N B E R G ▪ P H I L L I P S

A R C H I T E C T U R E

Randy Phillips, AIA

224 E. Douglas, Fifth floor   Wichita, KS 67202

Telephone 316.267.4002   Facsimile 316.267.1509

1. **A SMALL AD SHOP** （USA） Advertising 広告 CD, D: Traci Shiro AD: Richard Shiro DF: A Small Ad Shop

2. **WOOLF ARCHITECTS** （UK） Architecture 建築設計 AD, D: David Quay DF: David Quay Design

3. **SPANGENBERG PHILLIPS** （USA） Architecture 建築設計 CD, AD: Sonia Greteman D: Craig Tomson DF: Greteman Group

Uwe Steinmayer · Designer · agd/da
Seeheim 4 a · D-88131 Lindau/B
Tel. [+49.8382] 944 001
Isdn 944 002 · Fax. 4140

Uwe Steinmayer · Designer · agd/da
Seeheim 4 a · D-88131 Lindau/B
Tel. [+49.8382] 944 001
Isdn 944 002 · Fax. 4140

R A Y   H O N D A

451 PACIFIC AVENUE

SAN FRANCISCO

9   4   1   3   3

T: 415 705 6642

F: 415 705 6650

末広峰治

**S U E H I R O
M I N E J I
D E S I G N
O F F I C E**

末 広 峰 治 デザイン室
東京都目黒区中目黒3-12-16
クレール中目黒102 〒153
Telephone：03-5721-8823
Facsimile：03-5721-8824
(社)日本グラフィックデザイナー協会 会員

R A Y   H O N D A │ *D E S I G N*

T ▸ 707 762 6364 ◂ F

37 FAIRVIEW TERRACE PETALUMA CA 94952

JACK TOM
DESIGN

135 LAZY
BROOK RD.

MONROE
CT 06468

203
452-0889

1. **UWE STEINMAYER** （Germany）Designer デザイナー CD, AD, D: Uwe Steinmayer
2. **DMZ** （USA）Graphic design グラフィック デザイン D: Ray Honda DF: Ray Honda Design
3. **SUEHIRO MINEJI DESIGN OFFICE** （Japan）Graphic design グラフィック デザイン AD, D: Mineji Suehiro DF: Suehiro Mineji Design Office
4. **RAY HONDA DESIGN** （USA）Graphic design グラフィック デザイン CD, D: Ray Honda DF: Ray Honda Design
5. **JACK TOM DESIGN** （USA）Design デザイン CD, AD, D, I: Jack Tom DF: Jack Tom Design

1
2   3
4   5

1. **SURIC DESIGN** (Russia) Graphic design グラフィック デザイン AD, D, I: Yuri Surkov DF: Suric Design

2. **INGRID R. BUNN** (USA) Artist アーティスト CD, D, I, CW: Ingrid R. Bunn DF: I. B. Design Studio

3. **BALOH** (Slovenia) Carpet design カーペット デザイン CD, AD, D: Sašo Urukalo DF: Stvarnik d. j. j.

4. **SILVESTRI BÜRO FÜR INNENARCHITEKTUR** (Austria) Interior design インテリア デザイン CD, AD, D: Harry Metzler DF: Harry Metzler Artdesign

5. **IVAN ŠIJAK** (Yugoslavia) Photographer 写真家 CD, AD, D, I: Slavimir Stojanović DF: SMS Bates Saatchi & Saatchi Advertising Balkans

6. **EGO** (Slovenia) Fashion design ファッション デザイン CD: Metka Stvarnik AD, D: Sašo Urukalo DF: Stvarnik d. j. j.

1. **RADIATEUR FONTES** （France） Printing 印刷 CD, AD, D: Jean-Jacques Tachdjian DF: I Comme Image

2. **ANTONIO MERCADO** （USA） Photographer 写真家 CD, AD, D: José Serrano DF: Mires Design, Inc.

3. **PETER FLANAGAN PHOTOGRAPHY** （USA） Photography 写真 CD, AD, D: Karel Wöhlnick DF: Wöhlnick Design

4. **INDEPENDENT VISION** （USA） Lamp design ランプ デザイン CD, AD, D: Peat Jariya DF: Metal Studio Inc.

1 2
3 4

GLENN SWEITZER

Fresh Design

615/794-7708
FAX 615/794-5554
161 RIVERWOOD DRIVE
FRANKLIN, TENNESSEE 37069

1. **RICHARD KEHL** （USA） Illustrator　イラストレーター　CD, AD, D: Rick Eiber　I: Richard Kehl　DF: Rick Eiber Design
2. **FRESH DESIGN** （USA） Design　デザイン　D: Glenn Sweitzer　DF: Fresh Design
3. **REBECCA KEMPSTER** （Japan） Translator　翻訳家　D: Hiroshi Kuwamura　DF: Icono Grove

1

2　3

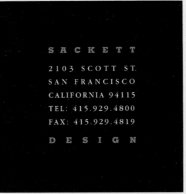

1. **SACKETT DESIGN ASSOCIATES** （USA） Graphic design　グラフィック デザイン　CD, AD, D: Mark Sackett　D: Wayne Sakamoto　DF: Sackett Design Associates

2. **SANDY GIN DESIGN** （USA） Graphic design　グラフィック デザイン　D: Sandy Gin　DF: Sandy Gin Design

3. **AXIA NEW MEDIA DESIGN** （USA） Design　デザイン　CD, AD, D: Petrula Vrontikis　CD: Lisa Levin　D: Christina Hsiao　DF: Axia New Media Design

4. **EDUARD ĆEHOVIN** （Slovenia） Design　デザイン　CD, AD, D: Eduard Ćehovin　DF: A±B

1 2
3
4

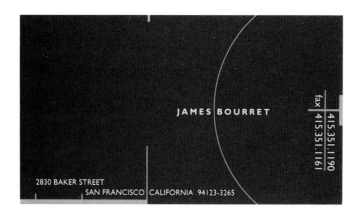

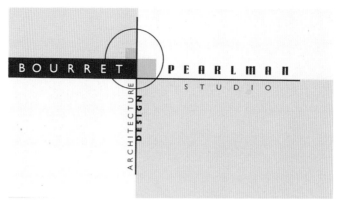

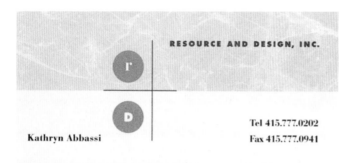

1. **BOURRET PEARLMAN**（USA）Architecture design　建築デザイン
CD, AD, D: Mark Sackett D: Wayne Sakamoto / James Sakamoto DF: Sackett Design Associates

2. **RESOURCE AND DESIGN, INC.**（USA）Interior design　インテリア デザイン　CD, AD, D, I: Mark Sackett D: Wayne Sakamoto DF: Sackett Design Associates

3. **MYRIAD DESIGN**（USA）Design　デザイン　CD, AD, D: Jane Cuthbertson DF: Myriad Design

1. **THE DESIGN FOUNDRY** （USA) Design デザイン CD, D: Jane Jenkins / Tom Jenkins DF: The Design Foundry
2. **THE DESIGN COMPANY** （USA) Graphic design グラフィック デザイン CD, AD, D: Marcia Romanuck DF: The Design Company

1

2

PAULA *Bee*
principal

PAULA *Bee* DESIGN
182 Costa Mesa Street
Costa Mesa
CALIFORNIA
9 2 6 2 7
fax 714 645 2003
714 548 0366

AI-D
501. 1-12-3 HIGASHI-SHINSAIBASHI.
CHUO-KU. OSAKA ZIP 542. JAPAN
TELEPHONE 06 251 5200
FACSIMILE 06 251 5466

伊達　徹
TORU DATE
MOBILE 030 71 44486

542
大阪市中央区
東心斎橋1-12-3
協栄ビル501 5F内

V
A
Joan Hix VanderSchuit
N
VanderSchuit
D
Studio Inc.
E
R
751 Turquoise
R
San Diego
S
California
C
92109-1034
H
Telephone
U
619-539-7337
I
Facsimile
T
619-539-2081

KODAMA KANZI

〒556大阪市浪速区
恵美須東1-5-14
メイト館302
TEL&FAX
06-644-6554

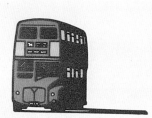

LONDON ROAD DESIGN

535 Ramona Street
Suite 33
Palo Alto
CA 94301

415 326 6103
Fax 415 326 6603

Jan Haseman

1. **PAULA BEE DESIGN** （USA）Graphic design **グラフィック デザイン** CD, AD, D, I: Paula Bee DF: Paula Bee Design
2. **AI-D** （Japan）Design **デザイン** CD, AD, D: Toru Date DF: AI-D
3. **VANDERSCHUIT STUDIO INC.** （USA）Photography **写真** CD, AD, D: José Serrano DF: Mires Design, Inc.
4. **KANZI KODAMA** （Japan）Artist **アーティスト** CD, AD, D: Sachi Sawada DF: Moss Design Unit
5. **LONDON ROAD DESIGN** （USA）Graphic design **グラフィック デザイン**
CD, D: Jan Haseman AD, D: Martin Haseman I: Michael Schwab DF: London Road Design

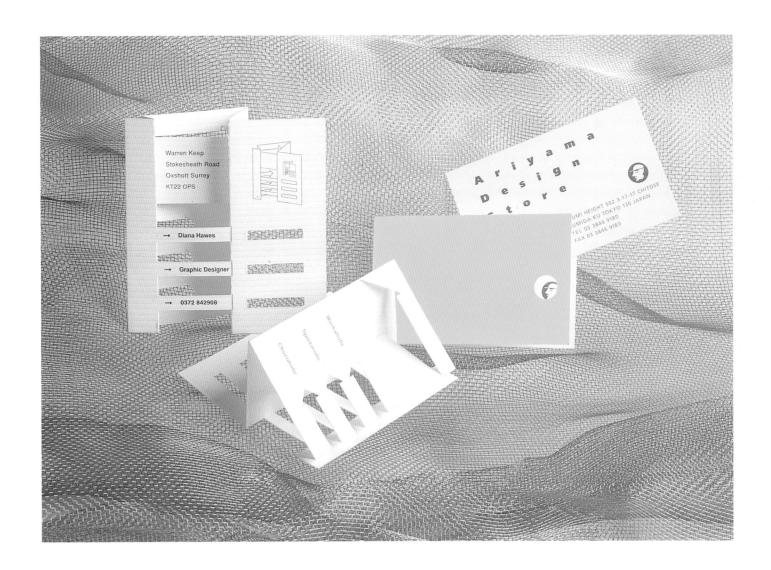

1. **DINA SHOHAM DESIGN STUDIO**　(Israel)　Graphic design　グラフィック デザイン　D: Dina Shoham

2. **HARTMUT SCHAARSCHMIDT**　(Germany)　Graphic designer　グラフィック デザイナー　CD, AD, D: Hartmut Schaarschmidt

3. **DIANA HAWES**　(UK)　Graphic designer　グラフィック デザイナー　D, I: Diana Hawes　DF: Diana Hawes Graphic Design

4. **ARIYAMA DESIGN STORE**　(Japan)　Graphic design　グラフィック デザイン　CD, AD, D, I: Tatsuya Ariyama

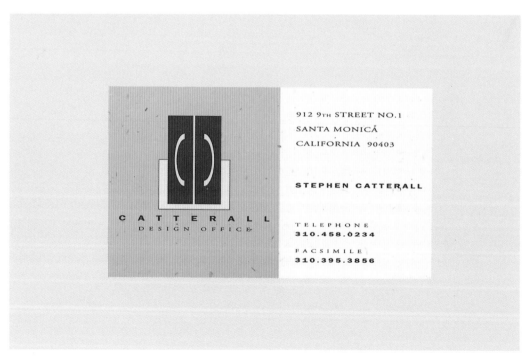

1. **NAOMI MURAKAMI** （Japan）Interior designer　インテリア デザイナー　AD, D: Masako Ban
2. **MASAKO BAN** （Japan）Graphic designer　グラフィック デザイナー　AD, D: Masako Ban
3. **EMANUEL BARBOSA DESIGN** （Portugal）Design　デザイン　CD, AD, D: Emanuel Barbosa　DF: Emanuel Barbosa Design
4. **STEPHEN CATTERALL** （USA）Interior designer　インテリア デザイナー　CD, AD, D: Petrula Vrontikis　DF: Vrontikis Design Office

TONY RINALDO PHOTOGRAPHY ► POST OFFICE BOX 559 ► CONCORD

MASSACHUSETTS 01742 ► TEL. 508.897.8104 ► FAX. 508.897.0650

MARIANNE MITTEN / **MITTEN DESIGN**

604 MISSION № 820 SAN FRANCISCO, CALIFORNIA 94105

TELEPHONE: **415.896.5386** FACSIMILE: **415.896.5387**

Aya Yamashiro
山 城 亜 矢

Tel & Fax 06 698 4441
Mobile 030 846 9714

アビス

558
大阪市住吉区
我孫子東2-7-13
ロイヤルキタノ1002号

 ABISS

Art Director
藤井克之
KATSUYUKI FUJII

Advertising Office
PLANET Inc.

有限会社 プラネット
京都市中京区両替町通御池下ル
ふじビル3F・4F 〒604
Phone(075)231-2522 Fax(075)252-5303

グラフィックデザイナー
日出真司

日出真司図案室

130 東京都墨田区吾妻橋

3-6-16-304

Tel./Fax.03-3623-1529

1. **TONY RINALDO PHOTOGRAPHY** (USA) Photography 写真 CD, AD, D: Karin Fickett DF: Plus Design Inc.
2. **MITTEN DESIGN** (USA) Graphic design グラフィック デザイン CD, AD, D: Marianne Mitten DF: Mitten Design
3. **ABISS** (Japan) Copywriting コピーライター CD: Aya Yamashiro AD, D: Toru Date DF: AI-D
4. **PLANET INC.** (Japan) Graphic design グラフィック デザイン CD: Katsuyuki Fujii D: Hizuru Kunitomo DF: Planet Inc.
5. **SHINJI HINODE ZUAN** (Japan) Graphic design グラフィック デザイン D: Shinji Hinode DF: Shinji Hinode Zuan

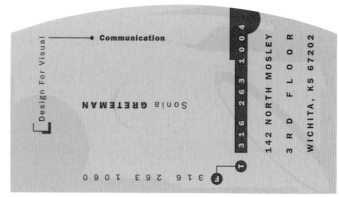

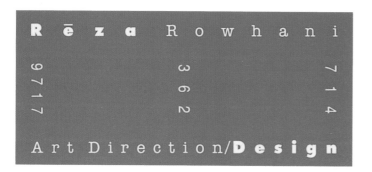

1. **GRETEMAN GROUP** （USA） Graphic design　グラフィック デザイン　CD, AD: Sonia Greteman　D: James Strange　DF: Greteman Group

2. **TODDESIGN** （USA） Design　デザイン　CD, D: Todd Simmons　DF: Toddesign

3. **REZA ROWHANI** （USA） Graphic designer　グラフィック デザイナー　CD, AD, D: Reza Rowhani　DF: Reza Rowhani Design

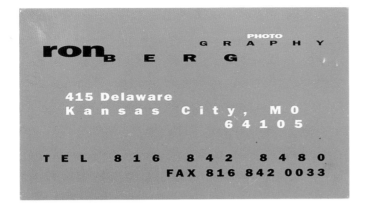

Level 1, 77a Acland Street, St Kilda, Victoria

P.O. Box 1107, St Kilda South, Victoria 3182, Australia

Telephone (03) 9537 1822

Facsimile (03) 9537 1833

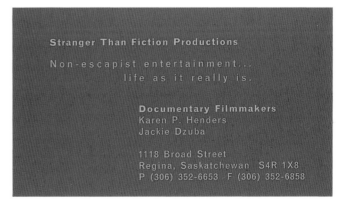

1. **RON BERG** （USA） Photographer 写真家 CD, AD: Sonia Greteman D: Jo Quillin / James Strange DF: Greteman Group

2. **ANDREW HOYNE DESIGN** （Australia） Design デザイン AD, D: Andrew Hoyne P: Marcus Struzina DF: Andrew Hoyne Design

3. **STRANGER THAN FICTION** （Canada） Film production 映画制作 AD, D: Catharine Bradbury P: Saskatchewan Archives DF: Bradbury Design Inc.

1
2
3

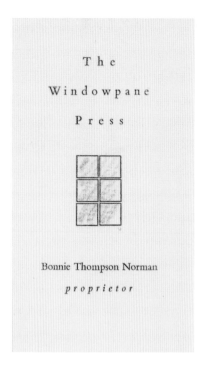

1. **KAORU MIYAZAKI** （Japan） Graphic designer グラフィック デザイナー　D: Kaoru Miyazaki

2. **THE WINDOWPANE PRESS** （USA） Printing 印刷　CD, AD, D, CW: Bonnie Thompson Norman　DF: The Windowpane Press

3. **KEN GRETEMAN** （USA） Photographer 写真家　CD, AD, D: Sonia Greteman　DF: Greteman Group

4. **KUNIHARU FUJIMOTO** （Japan） Photographer 写真家　D: Kazuo Abe　P: Kuniharu Fujimoto

5. **CHAPMAN-WINTER DESIGN** （USA） Design デザイン　CD, AD, D: Becky Chapman-Winter　DF: Chapman-Winter Design

6. **AFTER MIDNIGHT, INC.** （USA） Design デザイン　CD: Kathryn Klein　D, I: Tim McGrath　D: Maite Tone　DF: After Midnight, Inc.

1 2 3
4 5 6

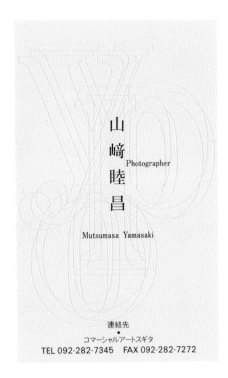

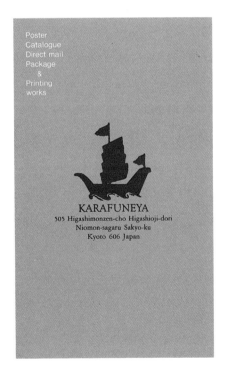

1. **BELYEA DESIGN ALLIANCE** （USA） Graphic design グラフィック デザイン CD, AD: Patricia Belyea D: Adrianna Jumping Eagle
GD: Brian O'Neill I: Jani Drewfs Color palettes: Samantha Hunt DF: Belyea Design Alliance

2. **MUTSUMASA YAMASAKI** （Japan） Photographer 写真家 CD, AD, D: Naoki Hirai DF: Creative Work Natural

3. **HITOMI YAMADA** （Japan） Illustrator イラストレーター AD, D: Isamu Nakazawa DF: Hi Hat Studio

4. **KATSUJI YAMADA** （Japan） Illustrator イラストレーター AD, D: Isamu Nakazawa DF: Hi Hat Studio

5. **KARAFUNEYA CO., LTD.** （Japan） Printing 印刷 AD, D: Sumihiro Takeuchi DF: Sumihiro Takeuchi Design Office

6. **MARK WOOD DESIGN OFFICE** （USA） Graphic design グラフィック デザイン CD, D: Mark Wood DF: Mark Wood Design Office

1 2 3
4 5 6

1. **PLUS DESIGN INC.** （USA） Design デザイン CD, AD, D: Anita Meyer / Karin Fickett
D: Dina Zaccagnini / Matthew Monk / Nicole Juen / Carolina Senior / Veronica Majlona DF: Plus Design Inc.

2. **MAHLUM & NORDFORS McKINELY GORDON** （USA） Architecture 建築設計
AD, D: Jack Anderson D: Leo Raymundo / Scott Eggers DF: Hornall Anderson Design Works, Inc.

3. **ROBERT A. ALEJANDRO ART AND DESIGN** Philippines Design デザイン CD, AD, D, I, CW: Robert A. Alejandro

4. **VESNA PAVLOVIĆ** （Yugoslavia） Photographer 写真家 CD, AD, D, CW: Škart DF: Škart Group

5. **STUDIO KON / STRUKTUR** （USA） Graphic design グラフィック デザイン CD, AD, D: Marc Hohmann / Akiko Tsuji DF: Studio Kon / Struktur

1 2
3 4
5

1. **ENZO PRESLEY INK DESIGN** （Australia） Stationery design　文具デザイン　AD, D: Andrew Hoyne　DF: Andrew Hoyne Design

2. **RAYMOND GRABER PHOTOGRAPHY** （USA） Photography　写真　AD, D: Keith C. Humphrey　DF: KCH Design

3. **ORBIT WEARABLES** （USA） T-shirt design　T-シャツ デザイン　CD, D: Molly J. Zakrajsek　CD, D: Patty J. Palazzo　DF: Triple Seven Design

4. **MIRES DESIGN, INC.** （USA） Graphic design　グラフィック デザイン　CD, AD, D: John Ball　Letterpress: Hal Truschke　DF: Mires Design, Inc.

5. **ANDY'S HOME ON THE RANGE** （Australia） Homeware design　生活雑貨デザイン　AD, D: Andrew Hoyne　I: Dean Gorissen　DF: Andrew Hoyne Design

6. **HIROSUKE UENO** （Japan） Illustrator　イラストレーター　AD: Hirosuke Ueno

```
1  2
3  4
5  6
```

1. **MODERN DOG** (USA) Design デザイン CD, AD, D, I: Robynne Raye DF: Modern Dog

2. **MODERN DOG** (USA) Design デザイン CD, AD, D, CW: Michael Strassburger DF: Modern Dog

3. **MODERN DOG** (USA) Design デザイン CD, AD, D, I, CW: George Estrada DF: Modern Dog

4. **MODERN DOG** (USA) Design デザイン CD, AD, D, CW: Michael Strassburger DF: Modern Dog

5. **MODERN DOG** (USA) Design デザイン CD, AD, D: Michael Strassburger DF: Modern Dog

1. **BOLT** （Japan) Design **デザイン** CD, AD, D: Sachi Sawada DF: Moss Design Unit

2. **BÜRO FÜR KOMMUNIKATIONSDESIGN** （Germany) Design **デザイン** CD, D: Detlef Behr DF: Büro für Kommunikationsdesign

3. **TE><TE** （Austria) Copywriter **コピーライター** CD, AD, D: Sigi Ramoser

photographer

市川 法子

〒158 世田谷区等々力3-25-12 #102

5706-4655

△TELEPHONE✕FACSIMILE▷**3704-8639**

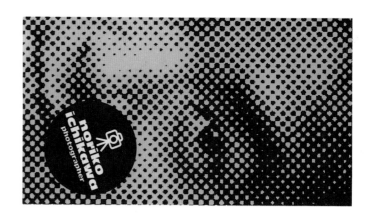

ウエハース
デザインチーム

スギウラ ユーコ
WAFERS DESIGN TEAM

渋谷区恵比寿2-37-8恵比寿ヂョイフル203

**TEL
FAX**▼**3447-5740**

馬場写真
BABA PHOTOGRAPH OFFICE & STUDIO
事務所

202 EBISU-BLDG.
1-8-14 EBISU
SHIBUYA-KU TOKYO
JAPAN 150
PHONE/FAX
03-3280-3081

日本広告写真家協会会員

PHOTOGRAPHER

馬場道浩
MICHIHARU BABA

馬場写真事務所
〒150 東京都渋谷区恵比寿1-8-14 恵比寿ビル202
TEL/FAX.03(3280)3081

1. **NORIKO ICHIKAWA**（Japan）Photographer 写真家 AD, D: Koichi Takahashi / Yuko Sugiura P: Noriko Ichikawa DF: Wafers Design Team
2. **WAFERS DESIGN TEAM**（Japan）Graphic design グラフィック デザイン AD, D: Koichi Takahashi / Yuko Sugiura DF: Wafers Design Team
3. **MICHIHARU BABA**（Japan）Photographer 写真家 D: Miki Takeshita

1
2
3

KING
TERRY SERVICE.

No Limit & No Retail Products.

™

KING TERRY SERVISE®
Published by FLAMINGO STUDIO, INC.
©1995 T.J.D. & D.J.C & Gang Rock & Many mo
For T-Back Agency. All rights reserved.
Unauthorized Duplication is Prohibited By Law.

FLAMINGO STUDIO. INCORPORATED

TO FRI. 13:00 - 17:00

● CREATIVE DIRECTION
● ADVERTISING
● MARCHANDICE PLANN
● GRAPHIC DESIGN
● EDITORIAL
● ILLUSTRATION

DONNY JORDAN

G-DESIGNER

PHONE
3352-9717
FAX
3354-1767

DONNY JORDAN.
CONNECTION®

A BOMB ASS GIFT
4 Tha G'z-Badd boyz & Hustla$

©Tara

Tha Tarantula® Production.   All rights reserved.

FLAMINGO STUDIO INCORPORATED®

HIROSHI KUROSAKA - DESIGNER

Open On Certain Holidays - Please Call
6-3-10 SHINJUKU, SHINJUKU-KU,
TOKYO,JAPAN, ZIP 160
CALL: **(03) 3352-9717** FAX: **(03) 3354-1767**

● **GRAPHIC DESIGN**
● **ILLUSTRATION**
● **CREATIVE DIRECTION**
● **MERCHANDISE PLANNING**

NOW WE WANT NEW BUSINESS !

™

MISTER TEE JAY
IN GOLDEN SMILE

FLAMINGO STUDIO.INC

1995
T.J.D.

©1995 Terry Johnson
for T-back Agency.
Unauthorized duplication
will git yo ass kicked!

FLAMINGO STUDIO.INC

Masahiro Inoue

6-3-10 Shinjuku Shinjuku-ku
Tokyo 160 Japan
Phone No. (03)3352-9717
Facsimile (03)3354-1767
Illustration (Terry Johnson,Tara)
Graphic Design-Creative Direction
Advertising - Editorial Design
Marchandise Planning-SK8orDie

Gang
ROCK™

1994
T.J.D

1. **FLAMINGO STUDIO INC.** （Japan) Graphic design グラフィック デザイン D: Donny Jordan I: Terry Johnson DF: Flamingo Studio Inc.

2. **FLAMINGO STUDIO INC.** （Japan) Graphic design グラフィック デザイン D: Donny Jordan DF: Flamingo Studio Inc.

3. **FLAMINGO STUDIO INC.** （Japan) Graphic design グラフィック デザイン D: Donny Jordan I: Tara DF: Flamingo Studio Inc.

4. **FLAMINGO STUDIO INC.** （Japan) Graphic design グラフィック デザイン D: Hiroshi Kurosaka DF: Flamingo Studio Inc.

5. **FLAMINGO STUDIO INC.** （Japan) Graphic design グラフィック デザイン D: Gangstarock® DF: Flamingo Studio Inc.

6. **FLAMINGO STUDIO INC.** （Japan) Graphic design グラフィック デザイン D: Gangrock （B.N.P ™) DF: Flamingo Studio Inc.

1 2 3
4 5
6

1. **RM BRÜNZ STUDIO** （USA） Graphic design グラフィック デザイン D, I: Robert M. Brünz DF: RM Brünz Studio

2. **MAURIZIO DELLA NAVE** Italy Graphic designer グラフィック デザイナー AD, D, DF: Maurizio Della Nave

3. **ESKIND WADDELL** （Canada） Graphic design グラフィック デザイン AD: Roslyn Eskind / Malcolm Waddell D: Nicola Lyon DF: Eskind Wadell

1

2 3

1. **GERMERSHEIM** （USA） Display production ディスプレイ制作 AD: Donna Johnston D: Kannex Fung DF: Finished Art Inc.

2. **ART STUFF** （USA） Design デザイン CD, AD, D, CW: Ellie Leacock P: Betsy Leacock DF: Art Stuff

1

2

グラフィック・デザイナー

大久保福祉

東京都渋谷区千駄ヶ谷二-二十四-五
コージーハウス二〇一 〒一五一
電話・ファックス〇三-三四七九・四三〇八

IAN McINNES
ADVERTISING CONCEPTS AND COPY

TELEPHONE
071 379 3434 OR 0799 550 583
FAX 0799 550 614

THE OLD VICARAGE · CLAVERING · SAFFRON WALDEN · ESSEX · CB11 4PQ

栫 秀二
Graphic Designer
SHUJI KAKOI

K's PROJECT · TOPORO 15·5F, 2-10-11, NISHISHINSAIBASHI, CHUOKU, OSAKA. 〒542
☎06-212-4166 ☎06-212-4008

吉田 勝

郵便番号二七二
千葉県市川市大和田
三丁目十九番十一号
フレンズハイム一〇三
電話・ファックス
〇四七三-七八-一〇八六

(masaru yoshida)
friends heim 103,
3-19-11
owada ichikawa-shi
chiba 272 japan
phone & fax:
0473-78-1086

Rill & Associates Architects, P.C.

Anne Y.S. Decker, AIA

4901 Fairmont Avenue
Suite 202
Bethesda, MD 20814

301.652.2484 PHONE
301.652.9262 FAX

TETSUZO

Art Director
佐藤直樹
SATO NAOKI

151 東京都渋谷区幡ヶ谷 2-24-1 遠山ビル 501
#501 Toyama Bldg., 2-24-1, Hatagaya, Shibuya-ku, Tokyo 151

鐵藏企画制作室
Tel & Fax 03-3378-0412

1. **FUKUSHI OKUBO** （Japan） Graphic designer　グラフィック デザイナー　AD, D: Fukushi Okubo　DF: Fukushi Okubo Design Office

2. **IAN McINNES** （UK） Copywriter　コピーライター　CD, AD, D: John Nash　DF: John Nash & Friends

3. **K'S PROJECT** （Japan） Graphic design　グラフィック デザイン　D: Shuji Kakoi　DF: K's Project

4. **MASARU YOSHIDA** （Japan） Designer　デザイナー　AD, D: Masaru Yoshida

5. **RILL & ASSOCIATES ARCHITECTS, P. C.** （USA） Architecture　建築設計
AD: Samuel G. Shelton / Jeffrey S. Fabian　D: Mimi Massé　DF: Kinetik Communication Graphics, Inc.

6. **TETSUZO** （Japan） Graphic design　グラフィック デザイン　AD, D: Naoki Sato　DF: Tetsuzo

友枝
雄策

Central Heights 2F, 5-20 Kamitori Machi,
Kumamoto-City, Japan 860
Phone 096・322・6167 Fax 096・325・7017

ARIMA DONYA, Inc.

154 東京都世田谷区
駒沢2-8-9 ♯302
TEL.(03) 3418-7519
FAX.(03) 3418-7568

Designer

内海彰

スタジオ タビィ
西宮市川西町7-30西号
〒662
Tel&Fax.0798・36・0409

Illustrator
上林宏明
Hiroaki Kambayashi

STUDIO TABBY[tǽbi]

洋画家

斎藤由比

150東京都渋谷区神宮前6-16-12-703
Tel 03-3409-7776

石川源（みなと）

FAX.03-3760-7588
TEL.03-3760-7591
中目黒4-12-7-503
〒153 東京都目黒区
石川源事務所

内海彰

graphic designer
UTSUMI, Akira

B-201, 7-24-19 KITAMI
SETAGAYA TOKYO 157 JAPAN
TEL.FAX.(03)3749-2805

157 世田谷区喜多見7-24-19, B-201

---

1. **YUSAKU TOMOEDA** （Japan） Graphic designer グラフィック デザイナー AD, D: Yusaku Tomoeda DF: Tomoeda Yusaku Design Office
2. **ARIMA DONYA, INC.** （Japan） Design デザイン AD, D: Akira Utsumi
3. **STUDIO TABBY** （Japan） Illustration イラストレーション CD: Masayuki Murakami D: Rie Morita I: Hiroaki Kambayashi DF: Creative Studio Bee Flight
4. **YUI SAITO** （Japan） Artist アーティスト D: Akihiko Tsukamoto
5. **MINATO ISHIKAWA ASSOCIATES INC.** （Japan） Graphic design グラフィック デザイン CD, AD, D: Minato Ishikawa DF: Minato Ishikawa Associates Inc.
6. **AKIRA UTSUMI** （Japan） Graphic designer グラフィック デザイナー AD, D: Akira Utsumi

1 2 3
4 5 6

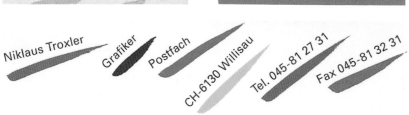

1. **ICEHOUSE DESIGN** （USA） Graphic design グラフィック デザイン CD: Pattie Belle Hastings AD, D: Bjorn Akselsen I: Val Tillery DF: Icehouse Design

2. **NIKLAUS TROXLER** （Switzerland） Designer デザイナー CD, AD, D, I, CW: Niklaus Troxler DF: Niklaus Troxler Design Studio

3. **BYBEE STUDIOS** （USA） Photography 写真 CD, AD, D: Mark Sackett D: James Sakamoto DF: Sackett Design Associates

1
2
3

ATELIER DESIGN
IDEIAILDA

GONÇALO

VILLA DE FREITAS

DESIGNER

20 2.º Dto

PORTUGAL

FONE 316 06 23
FAX 795 16 22

AV. SIDÓNIO PAIS,

1000 LISBOA

TELE

cristina trayfors productions

155 spring street third floor new york, 10012

tel 212 334 1500 fax 212 334 0106

cristina trayfors

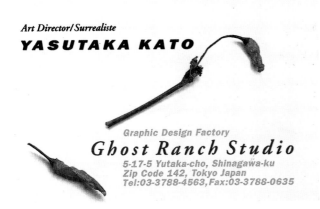

Art Director/ Surrealiste
YASUTAKA KATO

Graphic Design Factory
Ghost Ranch Studio
5-17-5 Yutaka-cho, Shinagawa-ku
Zip Code 142, Tokyo Japan
Tel:03-3788-4563, Fax:03-3788-0635

グラフィック・デザイン・ファクトリー：ゴースト・ランチ・スタジオ
〒142 東京都品川区豊町5丁目17番地5号
TEL：03-3788-4563, FAX：03-3788-0635

アートディレクター／シュールレアリスト
加藤 靖隆

© GRS.

Ghost Ranch Studio 5-17-5 Yutaka-cho, Shinagawa-ku, Tokyo 142, Japan
Telephone Number:03-3788-4563, Facsimile Number:03-3788-0635

Ghost Ranch Studio
yasutaka kato
Art Director

GRAPHIC DESIGN FACTORY

GHOST RANCH STUDIO

Art Director

加藤 靖隆

Yasutaka Kato

ゴースト・ランチ・スタジオ
〒142 東京都品川区豊町5-17-5
Telephone Number:03-3788-4563/ Facsimile Number:03-3788-0635

1. **IDEIA ILIMITADA** （Portugal） Graphic design **グラフィック デザイン** CD, D: Goncalo Falcão / Goncalo Freitas / Teresa Lago Da Silva DF: Ideia ilimitada

2. **CRISTINA TRAYFORS PRODUCTIONS** （USA） Artists **アーティスト** CD, AD, D: Robert Bergman-Ungar DF: Bergman-Ungar Associates

3. **GHOST RANCH STUDIO** （Japan） Graphic design **グラフィック デザイン** AD, D: Yasutaka Kato P: Ko Hosokawa DF: Ghost Ranch Studio

ARCHITECTURE

MICHEAL DOSS: STUDIO TELEPHONE: 206-270-9185

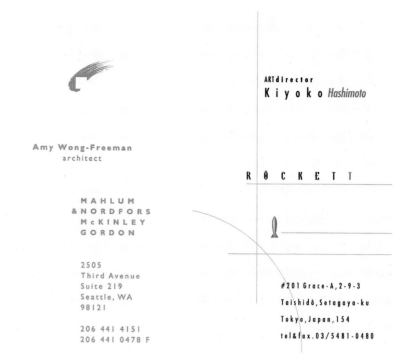

Amy Wong-Freeman
architect

MAHLUM
&NORDFORS
McKINLEY
GORDON

2505
Third Avenue
Suite 219
Seattle, WA
98121

206 441 4151
206 441 0478 F

ARTdirector
Kiyoko *Hashimoto*

RØCKETT

#201 Grace-A, 2-9-3

Taishidō, Setagaya-ku

Tokyo, Japan, 154

tel&fax.03/5481-0480

橋本 喜代子

〒154

東京都

世田谷区太子堂 2-9-3

グレースA #201

Tel & Fax.03/5481-0480

---

1. **MICHEAL O. DOSS** （USA） Architecture **建築設計** AD, D: Jack Anderson DF: Hornall Anderson Design Works, Inc.

2. **MAHLUM & NORDFORS McKINLEY GORDON** （USA） Architecture **建築設計**
AD, D: Jack Anderson D: Leo Raymundo / Scott Eggers DF: Hornall Anderson Design Works, Inc.

3. **KIYOKO HASHIMOTO** （Japan） Graphic designer **グラフィック デザイナー** D: Toshiyuki Yabana

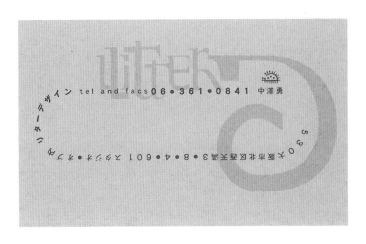

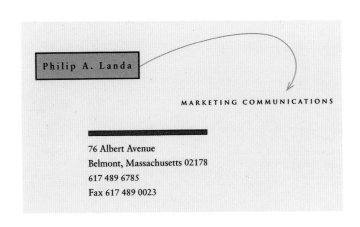

1. **D'SIGN & CO** （Germany） Design **デザイン** CD, AD, D: Doris Jausly / Claudia Ochsenbauer DF: D'sign & Co

2. **STIJLGROEP** （Netherlands） Architecture **建築設計** CD, AD, D: Limage Dangereuse

3. **TO BE DESIGNED** （USA） Design **デザイン** CD: Pat Garling AD, D: Eddie Segura P: Bruce Malone DF: To Be Designed

4. **ISAMU NAKAZAWA** （Japan） Graphic designer **グラフィック デザイナー** AD, D: Isamu Ñakazawa DF: Hi Hat Studio

5. **PHILIP A. LANDA** （USA） Copywriter **コピーライター** CD, AD, D: Jane Cuthbertson DF: Myriad Design

6. **A±B** （Yugoslavia） Design **デザイン** CD, AD, D: Edüard Ćehovin DF: A±B

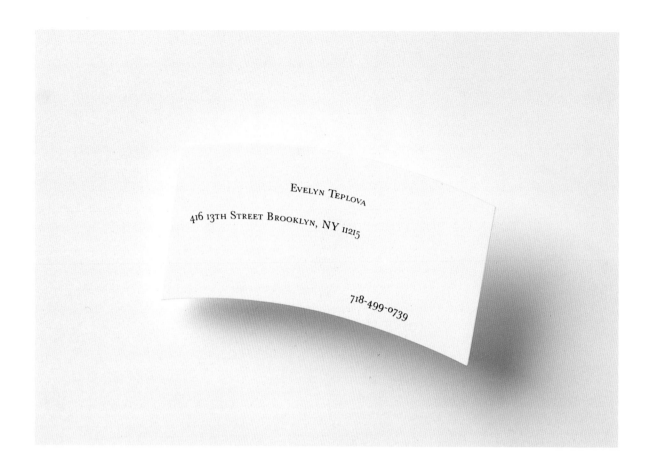

1. **EVELYN TEPLOVA DESIGN** （USA） Graphic design グラフィック デザイン CD, AD, D: Evelyn Teploff

2. **BRIAN MEREDITH** （USA） Copywriter コピーライター CD, AD, D: Scot Mires I: Seymour Chwast DF: Mires Design, Inc.

1

2

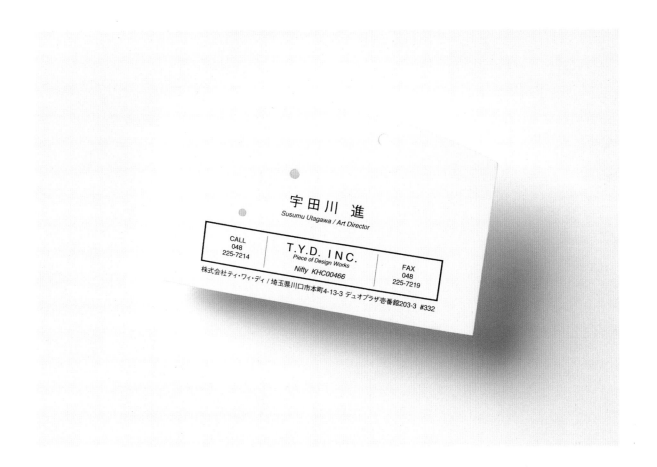

1. **T. Y. D. INC.** （Japan） Design **デザイン** AD: Tatsuaki Yasuno D: Susumu Utagawa DF: T. Y. D. Inc.

2. **LEONIDAS KANELLOS** （Greece） Designer **デザイナー** CD, AD, D: Leonidas Kanellos DF: Leonidas Kanellos Design Group

1
2

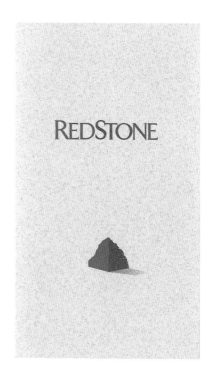

TETSUO FUJIWARA

Sepp Führer

Fotograf

Vordere Achmühle 24

A-6850 Dornbirn

Tel. 05572/23887

1. **STEREO STUDIO INC.** （Japan）Graphic design　グラフィック デザイン　AD, D: Tetsuo Fujiwara　DF: Stereo Studio Inc.

2. **SEPP FÜHRER** （Austria）Photographer　写真家　CD, AD, D, I: Sigi Ramoser

3. **RED STONE** （USA）Design　デザイン　CD, AD: Sonia Greteman　D: James Strange　DF: Greteman Group

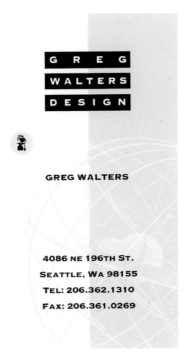

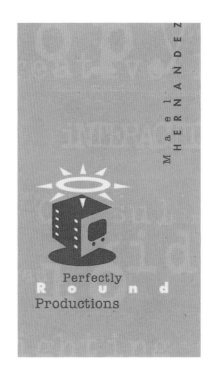

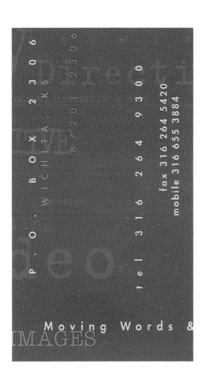

1. **GREG WALTERS DESIGN** （USA） Graphic design **グラフィック デザイン** CD, AD, D: Greg Walters DF: Greg Walters Design

2. **STREAMLINE GRAPHICS** （USA） Graphic design **グラフィック デザイン** CD, AD: Stan Evenson D: Glenn Sakamoto DF: Evenson Design Group

3. **PERFECTLY ROUND PRODUCTIONS** （USA） Video production **ビデオ制作** CD, AD, D: Sonia Greteman D: James Strange DF: Greteman Group

1
2
3

Rabuck/Carnie ADVERTISING INC.

BRIAN BURCHFIELD *Art Director*

3221 HUTCHINSON AVENUE, SUITE H

LOS ANGELES, CALIFORNIA 90034

Voice: 310 815 8225   *Fax:* 310 815 0770

Email: RCAadv@aol.com

1. **RABUCK / CARNIE ADVERTISING INC.** （USA) Advertising 広告 CD: Rick Rabuck AD, D, I: Brian Burchfield DF: Rabuck / Carnie Advertising, Inc.

2. **MACHUCA DESIGN** （USA) Graphic design グラフィック デザイン CD, D: Fred Machuca DF: Machuca Design

1

2

1. **CIARAN HUGHES** Ireland Designer デザイナー CD, AD, D, P, CW: Ciaran Hughes
2. **ORBIT WEARABLES** （USA） T-shirt Design T-シャツ デザイン CD, D: Patty J. Palazzo / Molly J. Zakrajsek DF: Triple Seven Design

1

2

de zeeuw
projekt realisatie

grafische vormgeving - illustratie - 3d design

Arie van Baarle

design consultant
communicatie adviezen

limage dangereuse r...
studio-adres pelgrimsstraat 3 - 3029 bn
telefoon 010 476 48 00 - fax 010 476 48 80
auto 06 52 73 86 43 - e-mail: limage @ knoware . nl

nederlandse vereniging van illustratoren nic
wethouder frankeweg 26 hs 1098 la amsterdam
tel 020-66 35 908 fax 020-66 35 915

(nic)

(nic)

1. **DE ZEEUW** （Netherlands）Garden architect 庭園設計 CD, AD, D: Limage Dangereuse
2. **LIMAGE DANGEREUSE BV** （Netherlands）Design デザイン CD, AD, D: Limage Dangereuse
3. **NIC** （Netherlands）Illustration イラストレーション CD, AD, D: Limage Dangereuse

1
2
3

PRINT NW / SIX SIGMA （USA） Printing 印刷 AD, D: Jack Anderson
D: Heidi Favour / Mary Chin Hutchison / Bruce Branson-Meyer DF: Hornall Anderson Design Works, Inc.

EUROPEAN
CREATIVE
HAND
BOOK
9 4 / 9 5

Rosie Prescott

International Sales Executive

**REED
INFORMATION
SERVICES**

Windsor Court
East Grinstead House
East Grinstead
West Sussex
RH19 1XA E

Tel +4
Fax
m

SINESS

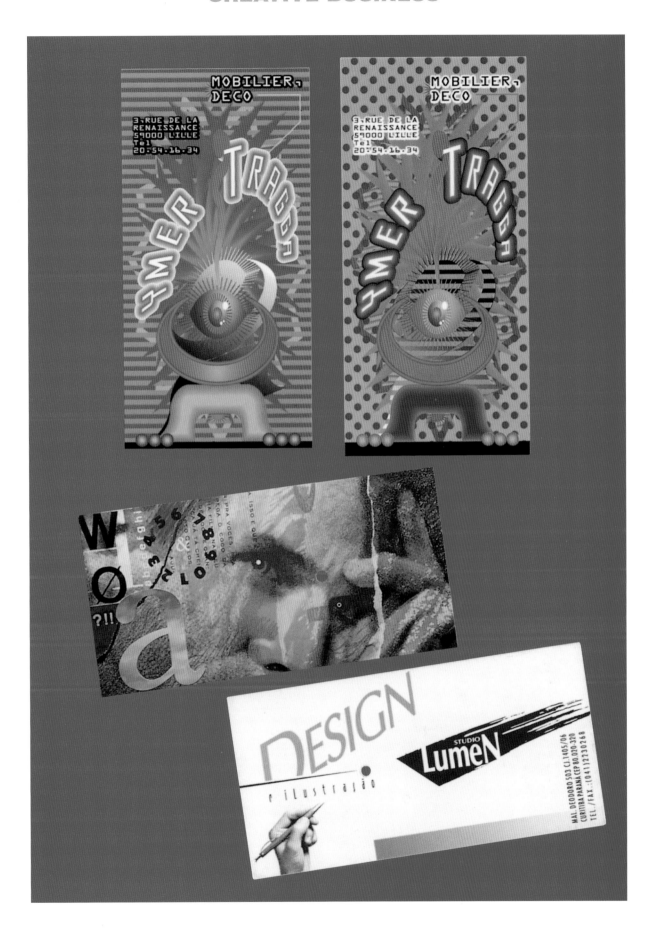

OPPOSITE PAGE: **REED INFORMATION SERVICES** （UK） Publisher 出版 CD, AD: Andy Ewan D: Anne Kristen Nybo P: Mann & Man DF: Design Narrative

1. **MOBILIER DECO** （France） Furniture design 家具デザイン CD, AD, D, I: Jean-Jacques Tachdjian DF: I Comme Image

2. **STUDIO LUMEN** （Brazil） Graphic design グラフィック デザイン CD, I: Silvio Silva Junior CD: Mirian Hatori

1

2

SEGURA 361 WES+ CHES+NU+ S+REE+, FIRS+ FL⊙⊙R, CHICAG⊙, ILLIN⊙IS 6⊙61⊙, USA. TEL 312.649.5688, FAX 312.649.⊙376, CEL 312.316.3564

1. **RIA SHIBAYAMA** （USA） Graphic designer グラフィック デザイナー CD, AD, D, P: Ria Shibayama
2. **TONI SCHOWALTER DESIGN** （USA） Graphic design グラフィック デザイン CD, AD, D: Toni Schowalter DF: Toni Schowalter Design
3. **GRAPHICAL POINT IZ** （Japan） Printing 印刷 CD, AD, D: Tomio Shinohara DF: Voice Corporation
4. **SEGURA INC.** （USA） Design デザイン CD, AD, D: Carlos Segura P: Greg Heck DF: Segura Inc.

1
2 3
4

Yoko Minakami

水上洋子

根津佳行

（荒川タカユキ）
郵便番号二四八
鎌倉市七里ヶ浜東
五丁目十一番三号
（湘南分室）
電話・ファックス
〇四六七三三一一四七三

（takayuki arakawa）
5-11-3
seven miles beach east,
kamakura-city,
kanagawa 248 japan
phone & fax:
0467-33-1473

272 千葉県市川市大和田3-19-1
フレンズハイム大和田103
phone 0473 78 1086

吉田 勝

山岡茂
東京都港区南青山5-15-9フラット青山305
Phone.3406-4551　Fax.3406-4969

吉田豊
Yutaka Yoshida

AD. Creators Group

【マトリックス】
大阪市北区天神橋1丁目18-25
第3マツイビル303号　ZIP530
phone.06-354-9083　fax.06-354-9084

1. **YOKO MINAKAMI** （Japan）Writer　ライター　D: Akihiko Tsukamoto
2. **TAKAYUKI ARAKAWA** （Japan）Copywriter　コピーライター　AD, D: Masaru Yoshida
3. **MASARU YOSHIDA** （Japan）Designer　デザイナー　AD, D: Masaru Yoshida
4. **STUDIO GIVE** （Japan）Graphic design　グラフィック デザイン　AD, D, DF: Studio Give
5. **MATRIX** （Japan）Graphic design　グラフィック デザイン　D: Yutaka Yoshida　DF: Matrix

1 2 3
4
5

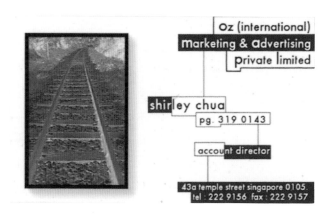

1. **REFLEX INC.** （Japan） Graphic design **グラフィック デザイン** CD, AD, D, I: You Kitagawa DF: Reflex Inc.

2. **INTERFACE SPIN CO., LTD.** （Japan） Design **デザイン** AD: Katsuhiro Masaki D: Gwenael Nicolas DF: Interface Spin Co., Ltd.

3. **OZ （INTERNATIONAL） MARKETING & ADVERTISING** Singapore Advertising **広告**
CD: Shirley Chua AD, P, I: Edmund Chia D: Daniel Chan CW: Amran Abdul Majid DF: Oz 《International》 Marketing & Advertising

4. **AL-HARF** Egypt Advertising **広告** CD: Mohsen Shaker AD: Mamdouh Salman D: Ahmed Attia I: Ahmed Al-essawy CW: Magdy Husein DF: Al-Harf

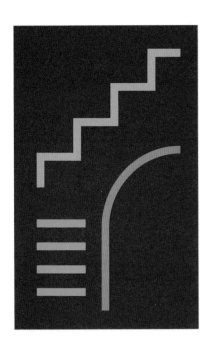

STATION NINETEEN
ARCHITECTS, INC.

DARREL LeBARRON, AIA
PARTNER

2001 UNIVERSITY
AVENUE SOUTHEAST
MINNEAPOLIS,
MINNESOTA 55414

612.623.1800
FAX 623.0012

ARCHITECTS,
PLANNERS,
INTERIORS

Grafica Design

Comunicazioni visive

Docente di Visual Design

Consulente e Trainer aziendale

di Creatività Costruttiva

Viale Libertà 89/B

20052 Monza MI - Italy

Telefono/fax 039.2026124

Vittorio Prina
Visual Designer

Vorklostergasse 60a
A-6900 Bregenz
Telefon 05574/47539
Fax 05574/47793

Paintbox
Telefon 05574/45677
Fax 05574/46734

1. **STATION 19 ARCHITECTS** （USA） Architecture design 建築デザイン CD, AD: John Reger D: Kobe DF: Design Center

2. **VITTORIO PRINA** （Italy） Designer デザイナー CD, AD, D: Vittorio Prina DF: Vittorio Prina Studio

3. **S. F. & H. FOTO STUDIO GMBH & CO.** （Austria） Photography 写真 CD, AD, D: Sigi Ramoser DF: Atelier für Text und Gestaltung

1. **SAM A. ANGELOFF** （USA） Copywriter コピーライター CD, AD, D: Rick Eiber CW: Sam A. Angeloff DF: Rick Eiber Design
2. **SLAVIMIR STOJANOVIĆ** （Yugoslavia） Designer デザイナー CD, AD, D, I: Slavimir Stojanović DF: SMS Bates Saatchi & Saatchi Advertising Balkans

1

2

1. **DIRK-DICE-SCHULZE** （Germany） Design **デザイン** D: Dice DF: Dice-Comixtrash & Geräuschkalotten
2. **SACKETT DESIGN ASSOCIATES** （USA） Graphic design **グラフィック デザイン** CD, AD, D: Mark Sackett D: Wayne Sakamoto DF: Sackett Design Associates

Phone 044-855-3964

YUMIKO OISHI

7-21-44 TSUCHIHASHI
KAWASAKI 213 JAPAN

CREA 20 352-D
RUA VICENTE MACHADO, 1771 · BATEL
TEL./FAX: (041) 243 6181
CEP 80440-020 · CURITIBA · PARANÁ

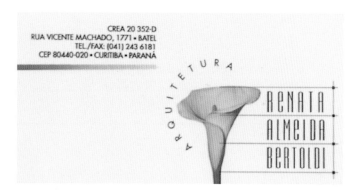

KELLY SPENCER

Thirty-one Robinwood Avenue
Jamaica Plain MA 02130 USA

phone fax 617 522 2001

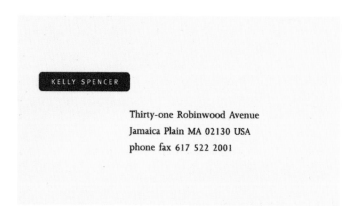

1. **YUMIKO OISHI** （Japan） Designer デザイナー D: Akira Takahashi DF: Básis Inc.

2. **MIKAKO HIROSE** （Japan） Graphic designer グラフィック デザイナー AD, D: Mikako Hirose

3. **RENATA BERTOLDI** （Brazil） Architecture 建築設計 CD, D: Silvio Silva Junior CD: Mirian Hatori DF: Studio Lumen Design

4. **FRESH DESIGN** （USA） Design デザイン D: Glenn Sweitzer DF: Fresh Design

5. **KELLY SPENCER** （USA） Copywriter コピーライター CD, AD, D: Jane Cuthbertson DF: Myriad Design

6. **TRACY SABIN GRAPHIC DESIGN** （USA） Graphic design グラフィック デザイン D, I: Tracy Sabin DF: Tracy Sabin Graphic Design

O TETSUYA H DESIGN T STUDIO A

SUN MINAMI-AOYAMA 303   3-14-14, MINAMI-AOYAMA MINATO-KU TOKYO 107, JAPAN
TEL. 03-479-3697 FAX. 03-479-6434

NIPPON DESIGN CENTER
Corporate Identity Division

Gaku Ohta
Art Director

Chuo Daiwa Bldg
1-13-13 Ginza, Chuo-ku,
Tokyo 104 Japan
Tel : 03-3567-3231
Fax : 03-3535-3569

BRÜCKE

株式会社ブリュッケ.
〒106東京都港区六本木5-13-1 101·201
BRÜCKE CO., LTD.
101·201, 5-13-1 Roppongi, Minato-ku
Tokyo106, Japan
Tel 03-3585-7181, Fax 03-3585-7049

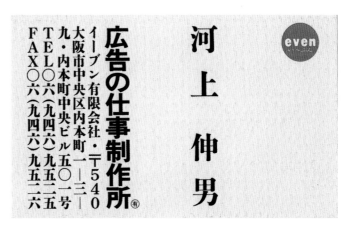

1. **TETSUYA OTA** （Japan） Graphic designer **グラフィック デザイナー** CD, AD, D: Tetsuya Ota

2. **THE NIPPON DESIGN CENTER** （Japan） Design **デザイン** AD, D: Gaku Ota DF: The Nippon Design Center Inc.

3. **JUMPING EAGLE DESIGN** （USA） Design **デザイン** CD, AD, D: Adrianna Jumping Eagle I: Gilbert Jumping Eagle DF: Jumping Eagle Design

4. **TAKESHI MATSUNAGA DESIGN OFFICE** （Japan） Graphic design **グラフィック デザイン** D: Takeshi Matsunaga

5. **BRÜCKE CO., LTD.** （Japan） Fashion design **ファッション デザイン** CD: Masaki Hoshino AD: Taki Ono

6. **ADVERTISING MAKER EVEN CO., LTD.** （Japan） Advertising **広告** CD: Nobuo Kawakami AD: Kazuo Kanosue DF: Advertising Maker Even Co., Ltd.

1 2
3 4
5 6

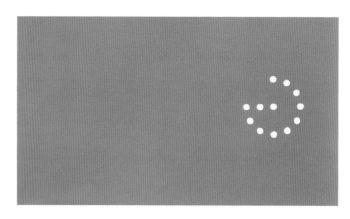

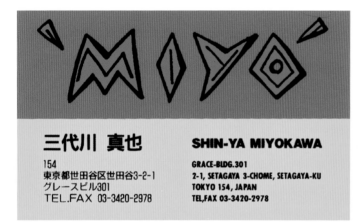

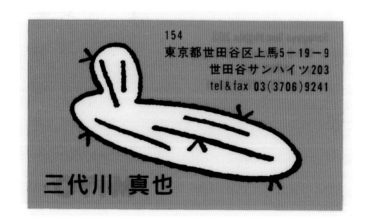

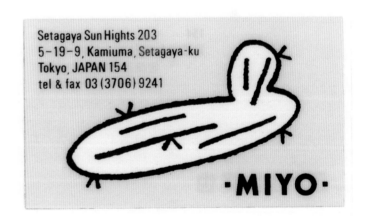

1. **PIERRE-YVES GOAVEC** （USA） Photographer 写真家 D: Erik Atigard / Patricia McShane DF: M. A. D.

2. **PHOTON FARMERS** （USA） Printing 印刷 CD, AD, D: Ellie Leacock DF: Art Stuff

3. **SHINYA MIYOKAWA** （Japan） Artist アーティスト D: Shinya Miyokawa

1
2
3

1. **REED INFORMATION SERVICES** (UK) Publisher 出版 CD, AD: Andy Ewan D: Anne Kristen Nybo DF: Design Narrative

1

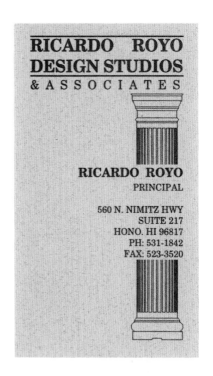

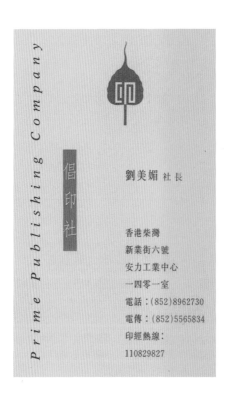

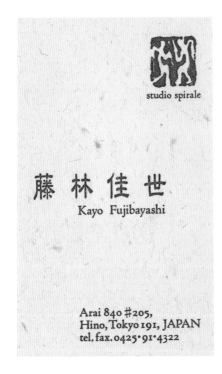

1. **RICARDO ROYO** （USA） Architecture 建築設計 CD, AD, D, I, CW: Lani Isherwood DF: La Visage
2. **NAM COMMUNICATION** （Japan） Advertising 広告 CD: Ippei Yunde D: Tsutomu Matsuda
3. **CREATIVE WORK NATURAL** （Japan） Design デザイン CD, AD, D: Naoki Hirai
4. **CIRO'S** （Japan） Graphic design グラフィック デザイン AD, D: Ciro Moritan
5. **PRIME PUBLISHING COMPANY** （Hong Kong） Publisher 出版 CD: Kan Tai-keung AD, D: Freeman Lau Siu Hong DF: Kan Tai-keung Design & Associates Ltd.
6. **KAYO FUJIBAYASHI** （Japan） Graphic designer グラフィック デザイナー D: Kayo Fujibayashi

1 2 3
4 5 6

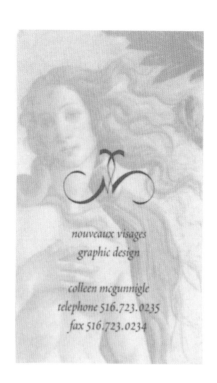

1. **AD LAND CO.,** （Japan）Advertising　広告　CD, AD, D: Hideo Yagi　DF: Yagi Design Room
2. **NOUVEAUX VISAGES**　（USA）Graphic design　グラフィック デザイン　D: Colleen McGunnigle　DF: Nouveaux Visages
3. **MITSUHIRO HASEGAWA**　（Japan）Graphic designer　グラフィック デザイナー　CD, AD, D, I: Mitsuhiro Hasegawa
4. **YAGI DESIGN ROOM**　（Japan）Graphic design　グラフィック デザイン　CD, AD, D: Hideo Yagi　DF: Yagi Design Room
5. **YOSHIOKA ART・N**　（Japan）Graphic design　グラフィック デザイン　CD, D: Kai Yoshioka　I: Ten Yoshioka
6. **KOKOKUNOJYO**　（Japan）Design　デザイン　AD, D: Hiroaki Konya　DF: Kokokunojyo

1. **KIRK WEDDLE PHOTOGRAPHY** (USA) Photography 写真 CD, AD, D: Tracy McGoldrick P: Kirk Weddle DF: Tracy Mac

2. **WB ADAMS** (USA) Publisher 出版 CD, AD, D: Takeshi Takahashi

3. **KEHRT SHATKEN SHARON ARCHITECTS** (USA) Architecture 建築設計
CD, AD, D: Roger Cook / Don Shanosky D: Douglas M. Baszczuk DF: Cook and Shanosky Associates, Inc.

4. **SOMA ARCHITECTS** (USA) Architecture 建築設計 AD, D: Samuel G. Shelton / Jeffrey S. Fabian D: Jean Kane DF: Kinetik Communication Graphics, Inc.

5. **GRAFX DESIGN** (USA) Graphic design *グラフィック デザイン* D, I: John Sparks DF: Grafx Design

6. **ASHLOR PUBLISHING** (USA) Publisher 出版 CD, AD, D, I: Jack Tom DF: Jack Tom Design

1 2
3 4
5 6

P   o   O   **POOL**   o   L

川
辺
京

専務取締役
小泉 敏夫

株式会社 プライム
〒223 横浜市港北区綱島東1-16-23
TEL. 045－544－9580
FAX. 045－546－3873

CORPORATE DESIGN & ARTWORK

PRIME
CORPORATION®

イラストレーター
中野邦彦

イメージハウス メディア

540　大阪市中央区上町1丁目20-15　TEL 06-763-1037　FAX 06-763-5819

Photographer
鵜飼茂一
Ugai, Moichi.

プレス・パシフィカ
東京都渋谷区恵比寿西2-3-11
メゾン・ド・エビス808 〒150
Phone and Facsimile
dial ; 03,3462,4636
Private phone and facsimle
dial ; 03,3469,6413.

PRESS o f o
Pacifica

Room Number 808, Maison De Ebis, 2-3-11, Ebis Nishi,
Shibuya-ku, Tokyo, Zip Code 150, Japan.

SIXth metal option #103,3-7-21,daikoku,naniwa-ku,osaka.556
phone:06.631.7625
ISHIHARA YASUHIRO

Sixth
METAL OPTION

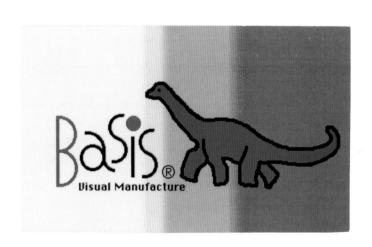

1. **KYO KAWABE** （Japan） Copywriter **コピーライター** D: Akihiko Tsukamoto

2. **LOGO FACTORY SECTION** （Japan） Graphic design **グラフィック デザイン** CD: Toshio Koizumi AD, D: Murray Swift DF: Prime Corporation

3. **KUNIHIKO NAKANO** （Japan） Photography **写真** D: Yukihiro Hirose DF: Image House Media

4. **PRESS PACIFICA** （Japan） Photography **写真** AD, D: Yoshihiro Madachi DF: Design Studio Waters

5. **SIXTH** （Japan） Chasing **彫金** CD, AD, D: Sachi Sawada DF: Moss Design Unit.

6. **BÁSIS INC.** （Japan） Design **デザイン** D, I: Akira Takahashi DF: Básis Inc.

1 2
3 4
5 6

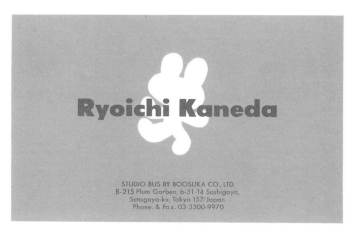

1. **AKIKO TAKASHIMA** （Japan）Designer **デザイナー** D, I: Akiko Takashima DF: Voice Corporation
2. **VISAGE CORPORATION** （Japan）Design **デザイン** AD, D: Mamoru Isobe
3. **CID LAB. INC.** （Japan）Design **デザイン** AD, D: Yukichi Takada DF: CID Lab. Inc.
4. **STUDIO BUS BY BOOSUKA** （Japan）Advertising **広告** D: Sonoko Kaneda I: Boosuka
5. **JUNKO UCHINO** （Japan）Designer **デザイナー** AD, D, I: Junko Uchino
6. **YOSHINOBU SAITO** （Japan）Illustrator **イラストレーター** AD, D, I: Yoshinobu Saito

1 2
3 4
5 6

1. **ICONO GROVE** （Japan） Design **デザイン** D: Hiroshi Kuwamura DF: Icono Grove

2. **EUAN CRAIG** （Japan） Potter **陶芸家** D: Douglas Doolittle DF: Douglas Design Inc.

3. **NEUTRAL CORPORATION** （Japan） Graphic design **グラフィック デザイン** CD, AD: Katsu Asano D: Kinue Yonezawa DF: ASA 100 Company

4. **BEFORE CHRIST** （Japan） Advertising **広告** AD, D: Junichi Naito DF: J・Family

5. **METAL STUDIO INC.** （USA） Design **デザイン** CD, AD, D: Peat Jariya D: Scott Head / Fotis Gerakis DF: Metal Studio Inc.

6. **MITSUHIRO HASEGAWA** （Japan） Designer **デザイナー** CD, AD, D, I: Mitsuhiro Hasegawa

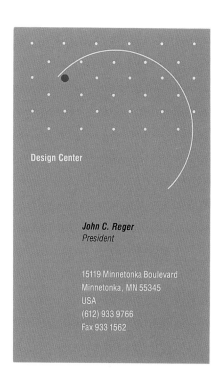

Design Center

John C. Reger
President

15119 Minnetonka Boulevard
Minnetonka, MN 55345
USA
(612) 933 9766
Fax 933 1562

荻野英朗

hideo ogino

小林健三デザイン室

03 3317 7696

105, 3-7-13, hamadayama
suginami-ku, tokyo
japan 168
杉並区浜田山

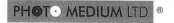

Czesław A. Czapliński
photojournalist

USA
tel./fax 718.389.9606
107 Milton Street, Brooklyn, New York 11222

Poland
tel./fax +22/621.65.08
ul. Natolińska 3 m.79, 00-562 Warszawa

CLIFFORD CHENG

VOICE
graphic + environmental design

1385 Alewa Drive
Honolulu, Hawai'i
96817-1511
T [808] 595-0040
P [808] 527-1666

BÍLL

代表取締役
President / Shozo Tsuda
津 田 昇 三

株式会社 ビル
〒550 大阪市西区南堀江3丁目16-4 ヴェスタ堀江205
06-539-1931(代)/Fax.06-539-1933

このシールを剝がしてアドレス帳にお貼りください。転記いただく手間が省けます。
【特許出願中】このシール名刺に関するお問い合わせは(株)ビルまで。

BÍLL　　株式会社ビル 津田昇三
〒550 大阪市西区南堀江3丁目16-4
ヴェスタ堀江205
06-539-1931(代)/Fax.06-539-1933

株式会社 ビル 津 田 昇 三
〒550 大阪市西区南堀江3丁目16-4 ヴェスタ堀江205
06-539-1931(代)/Fax.06-539-1933

AKIYAMA & CO.,

代表
秋 山 徹

〒150 東 京 都 渋 谷 区
神 宮 前 3 - 1 - 12
プリンスハイツ 103号
TEL:(03)3478-2105
FAX:(03)3478-2106

1. **KENZO KOBAYASHI DESIGN** （Japan）Graphic design グラフィック デザイン D: Kenzo Kobayashi DF: Kenzo Kobayashi Design
2. **DESIGN CENTER** （USA）Graphic design グラフィック デザイン CD, AD, D: John Reger D: Dick Stanley DF: Design Center
3. **BILL INC.** （Japan）Advertising 広告 CD: Shozo Tsuda AD, D: Kenji Nakai
4. **CZESLAW A. CZAPLINSKI** （Poland）Photographer 写真家 CD, AD, D: Tadeusz Piechura CW: Czeslaw A. Czaplinski DF: Atelier Tadeusz Piechura
5. **VOICE DESIGN** （USA）Design デザイン CD, AD, D: Clifford Cheng DF: Voice Design
6. **AKIYAMA & CO.,** （Japan）Design デザイン D: Toru Akiyama

1 2 3
4 5 6

編集部

磯 村　完

株式会社 **ケイオフィス**
〒151 東京都渋谷区西原3-1-10 金杉ビル301
Tel.03(485)7178 Fax.03(468)2442

企画部

友 滝 三 生

大阪市中央区谷町6丁目18-17 千田ビル 〒542　TEL.06·765·3921(代)　FAX.06·765·3923

801 LAPIZ KAKINUMA, 3-3-8, EBISU, SHIBUYA-KU, TOKYO. ZIP.150
TEL. 03-5420-0347　FAX. 03-5420-0348 ☻☀☮☺☯✝♁♰♇♉☾♂✹

O'Z Inc.

代表取締役

小 野 信 行

Nobuyuki ONO

 有限会社 オッズ

Telephone　06.771.0565
Facsimile　06.771.0557

543 大阪市天王寺区上本町8丁目7番1号 海老原ビル4F

YASUHIRO YASUTOMO

No.102 Azabukingdom
1-4-20 Nishi-Azabu
Minato-ku Tokyo Japan 106
TEL. 03(3423)0816
FAX. 03(3423)0708

埼玉県朝霞市西原1-8-7-403 〒351
Tel+fax:048-476-0772
Kazumasa Watanabe
Present Adress:
403,1-8-7 Nishihara, Asaka City,
Saitama Prefecture 351

渡邊一正 graphic designer

1. **K-OFFICE CO., LTD.**（Japan）Editing **編集** CD, AD, D: Tetsuya Ota
2. **ALPHA PRINTING CO., LTD.**（Japan）Printing **印刷** AD, D: Sansei Tomotaki
3. **NEWS CO., LTD.**（Japan）Photography **写真** CD, AD, D: Yukio Ikoma DF: I'm Co., Ltd.
4. **O'Z INC.**（Japan）Display production **ディスプレイ制作** CD, AD, D: Toru Date　DF: AI-D
5. **YASUHIRO YASUTOMO**（Japan）Photographer **写真家** CD, AD, D: Tetsuya Ota
6. **KAZUMASA WATANABE**（Japan）Graphic designer **グラフィック デザイナー** D: Kazumasa Watanabe

sal vergara art director
1120 rhode island san
francisco california 94107 tel
415.647.6507 fax 415.647.2482

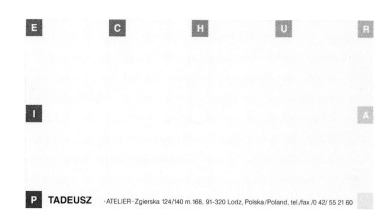

P **TADEUSZ** ·ATELIER· Zgierska 124/140 m.168, 91-320 Lodz, Polska/Poland, tel./fax /0 42/ 55 21 60

sigi ramoser
grafik designer da
t 05572/27481 f 27484

atelier für text und gestaltung
brändle dornig ramoser scherling oeg
a-6850 dornbirn sägerstraße 4

22, Saraswat Colony Near Zilla Parishad
Pune – 411 001. India
Phone : (0212) 64 5085 / 62 9277
Fax : (0212) 64 6650

122, Poornanand
62 Banganga Walkeshwar
Bombay – 400 006. India
Phone : 364 3743

AHA
PRACOWNIA ARCHITEKTURY
Jacek Bretsznajder ul. Wigury 28 m.17a, 90-319 Łódź, tel. 743000

Aileen Farnan Antonier

Copywriting

228 Main Street   for Business Communications

Venice. CA 90291

213/396-9596

FAX/396-7729

1. **SAL VERGARA** （USA） Design デザイン CD: Traci Shiro AD, D, I: Richard Shiro DF: A Small Ad Shop
2. **ATELIER TADEUSZ PIECHURA** （USA） Graphic design グラフィック デザイン CD, AD, D, CW: Tadeusz Piechura DF: Atelier Tadeusz Piechura
3. **ATELIER FÜR TEXT UND GESTALTUNG** （Austria） Design デザイン CD, AD, D: Sigi Ramoser DF: Atelier für Text und Gestaltung
4. **GURUDUTT** （India） Photography 写真 CD, AD, D: Sudarshan Dheer DF: Graphic Communication Concepts
5. **AHA-PRACOWNIA ARCHITEKTURY** （Poland） Architecture 建築設計 CD, AD, D, CW: Tadeusz Piechura CW: Jacek Bretsznajder DF: Atelier Tadeusz Piechura
6. **AILEEN FARMAN ANTONIER** （USA） Copywriter コピーライター CD, AD, D: Petrula Vrontikis DF: Vrontikis Design Office

1 2
3 4
5 6

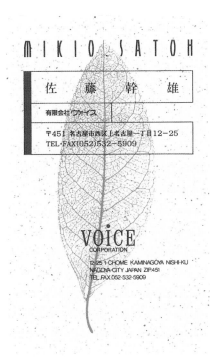

有限会社 エファウ
150 渋谷区恵比寿南2・4・4
恵比寿光洋ハイツ301号室
Phone:03・3793・9077
Fax:03・3793・9093

プロデューサー
植木健次

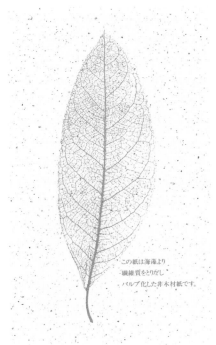

この紙は海藻より
繊維質をとりだし
パルプ化した井木村紙です。

Ueki Kenji
efaw Ltd.
2・4・4 Ebisu Minami, Shibuya-ku, Tokyo 150 Japan
Phone:03・3793・9077
Fax:03・3793・9093

〒456
名古屋市熱田区明野町4-10
☎ 052-681-5346

1. **VOICE CORPORATION** （Japan） Advertising **広告** CD, AD, D: Mikio Sato DF: Voice Corporation
2. **EFAW LTD.** （Japan） Design **デザイン** CD, AD, D, I: Hiroyoshi Kasuya DF: Efaw Ltd.
3. **MIKI SHINOHARA** （Japan） Illustrator **イラストレーター** CD: Tomio Shinohara AD, D, I: Miki Shinohara DF: Voice Corporation

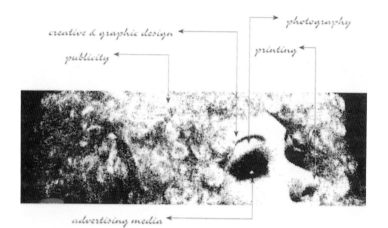

1. **JOHN T. STRAUSZ** （Canada） Illustrator イラストレーター CD, AD, D, I: John T. Strausz

2. **SIGI RAMOSER** （Austria） Graphic designer グラフィック デザイナー CD, AD, D: Sigi Ramoser I: Selina Ramoser

3. **EYE STUDIO LTD.** （Hong Kong） Advertising 広告 CD: Ching Lai Shan AD, D, P: Ng Kam Ming

4. **MARIKO** （Greece） Fashion design ファッション デザイン CD, AD, D: Leonidas Kanellos DF: Leonidas Kanellos Design Group

5. **KAWABATA DESIGN FACTORY** （Japan） Design デザイン AD, D: Kazuo Kawabata DF: Kawabata Design Factory

6. **ELICO MURAMATSU** （Japan） Designer デザイナー CD, AD, D, I, CW: Elico Muramatsu DF: k. m. p.

```
1 2
3 4
5 6
```

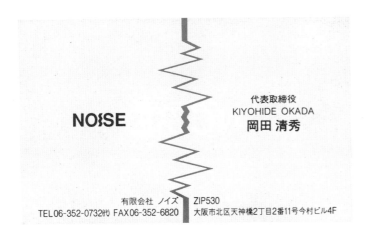

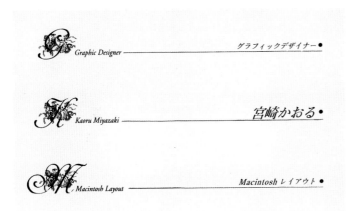

1. **NOISE** （Japan） Design **デザイン** D: Kaname Nakayama DF: Noise

2. **KAORU MIYAZAKI** （Japan） Graphic designer **グラフィック デザイナー** D: Kaoru Miyazaki

3. **SPOON CO., LTD.** （Japan） Illustration **イラストレーション** D: Juriko Saito I: Kunio Sato

安久利徳

180東京都武蔵野市吉祥寺本町2-32-18
ハイツ扇山
Tel 0422・22・0835　Fax 0422・22・0885

グラフィックデザイナー

原 紀子

〒361

行田市谷郷

2543

phone/fax 0485 54 7124

2543

Yagô Gyôda-city

Saitama, 361

Japan

graphic designer
Noriko HARA

高林 杏子
takabayashi yoko

郵便番号171 東京都豊島区目白4-5-3 ブランドール目白203
Telephone & Facsimile 03-5982-5956

1. **TOKU AGURI** （Japan）Illustrator **イラストレーター** D: Akihiko Tsukamoto
2. **NORIKO HARA** （Japan）Graphic designer **グラフィック デザイナー** AD, D: Noriko Hara D: Rentaro Harada
3. **YOKO TABABAYASHI** （Japan）Graphic designer **グラフィック デザイナー** AD, D: Jun Takechi

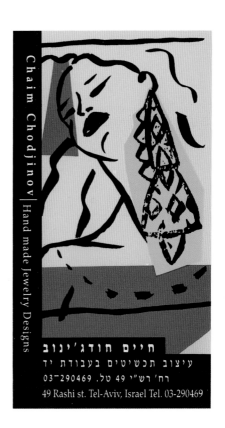

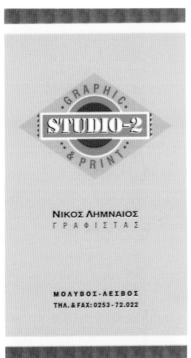

1. **D4TV** （USA）Advertising 広告 CD, AD, CW: Suzanne Hatfield CD, AD, CW: Bernard Klinger DF: D4TV （Design for Television）

2. **LEONIDAS KANELLOS** （Greece）Design デザイン CD, AD, D: Leonidas Kanellos DF: Leonidas Kanellos Design Group

3. **CHAIM CHODJINOV** （Israel）Jewelry designer ジュエリー デザイナー D, I: Dina Shoham

4. **STUDIO-2** （Greece）Graphic design グラフィック デザイン CD, AD, D: Leonidas Kanellos DF: Leonidas Kanellos Design Group

5. **MIKE SALISBURY COMMUNICATIONS, INC.** （USA）Graphic design グラフィック デザイン
   CD, AD: Mike Salisbury D: Regina Grosveld DF: Mike Salisbury Communications, Inc.

6. **GREG ELMS PHOTOGRAPHY** （Australia）Photography 写真 AD: Andrew Hoyne D: Andrew Hoyne Design I: Anton Orlowski DF: Andrew Hoyne Design

ATSUKO SHIMA
510-4, Hinokuchi, Matsudo-shi,
Chiba-ken, Japan
TEL.0473-60-1481 FAX.0473-60-1413

© ATSUKO SHIMA
PAPER WORK 1993

吉田デザイン事務所
PACKAGE DESIGN・GRAPHIC DESIGN

Designer 吉田朋子
TOMOKO YOSHIDA
〒146 東京都大田区池上4-16-6-103
TEL. FAX. 03-753-9516

dh
▲▲▲▲▲
Damion Hickman Design
Damion W. Hickman/Graphic Designer
Telephone:
(seven one four) four seven two - zero zero five two
Facsimile:
(seven one four) seven seven zero -six zero three one

TEL/FAX: 716/388-9532   PATTI J. LACHANCE

DUTCH MILL
D E S I G N
4 PELHAM
P A R K
FAIRPORT
NEW YORK
1 4 4 5 0

who da
thunk
it?!

maria baxter!?
615/228-0470!
p.o. box 68316
nashville, tn 37206

Prints/Greeting Cards/T-shirts

TOLOOPgraphics.
UNIT OSAKA GUERRILLA

制作
森永 悟
Satoru Morinaga
有限会社トゥールーブ・グラフィックス
大阪市西区川口町1-1-11
五琳ビル303号 〒550
telephone 06-581-9888
facsimile 06-581-9889

1. **ATSUKO SHIMA ART PRODUCTION** （Japan）Artist アーティスト D: Atsuko Shima P: Hiro Onodera DF: Atsuko Shima Art Production
2. **YOSHIDA DESIGN OFFICE** （Japan）Design デザイン D: Tomoko Yoshida
3. **DAMION HICKMAN DESIGN** （USA）Graphic design グラフィック デザイン D: Damion Hickman DF: Damion Hickman Design
4. **DUTCHMILL DESIGN** （USA）Graphic design グラフィック デザイン CD, AD, D: Patti J. Lachance DF: Dutchmill Design
5. **WHO DA THUNK IT ?!** （USA）Artist アーティスト D: Glenn Sweitzer P: Marla Baxter DF: Fresh Design
6. **TOLOOP GRAPHICS INC.** （Japan）Advertising 広告 CD, AD, D: Toloop Graphics Inc.

1 2 3
4 5 6

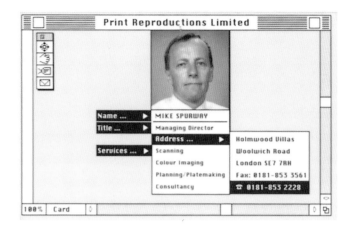

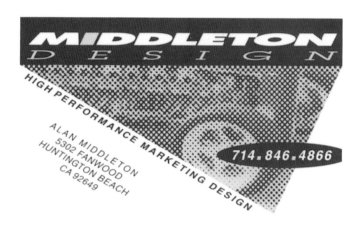

1. **PRINT REPRODUCTIONS** （UK） Printing 印刷 CD, AD, D: John Nash DF: John Nash & Friends

2. **DENNIS IRWIN ILLUSTRATION** （USA） Illustration イラストレーション AD: Andrew Danish D, I: Dennis Irwin

3. **DEAN PHIPPS** （Australia） Photographer 写真家 AD, D: Andrew Hoyne P: Dean Phipps DF: Andrew Hoyne Design

4. **MIDDLETON PERFORMANCE MARKETING** （USA） Design デザイン
CD, AD, D, I, CW: Alan Middleton P: Goodguy's Magazine staff photo DF: Middleton Performance Marketing

5. **PROTHESIS LTD.** （Greece） Design デザイン CD, AD, D: Leonidas Kanellos DF: Leonidas Kanellos Design Group

6. **JUN NAGASHIMA** （Japan） Designer デザイナー AD, D: Jun Nagashima

1 2
3 4
5 6

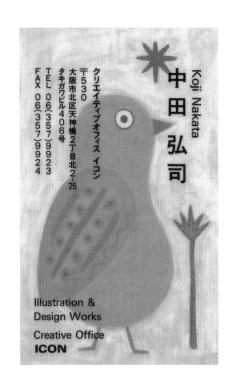

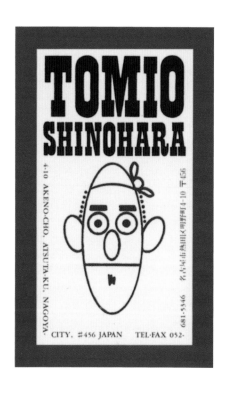

1. **SD FACTORY** （Japan） Architecture 建築設計 AD, D: Fukushi Okubo DF: Fukushi Okubo Design Office
2. **CREATIVE OFFICE ICON** （Japan） Design デザイン D, I: Koji Nakata DF: Creative Office Icon
3. **MACHIE TORII** （Japan） Designer デザイナー CD, AD, D, I: Machie Torii P: Akio Magario P: Izumi Takahashi
4. **MIYAMOTO DESIGN OFFICE** （Japan） Graphic design グラフィック デザイン CD, AD, D: Taketo Miyamoto
5. **TOMIO SHINOHARA** （Japan） Designer デザイナー CD, AD, D, I: Tomio Shinohara DF: Voice Corporation
6. **TAKASHI IWAKIRI** （Japan） Photographer 写真家 AD, D: Takeo Aizawa （Alfalfa）

Nigel Holmes

544 Riverside
Avenue
Westport
CT 06880
USA

Phone **203-226-2313**
Fax **203-222-9545**
nigelholme @ aol.com

MARTTI LUNDSTRÖM

Kirjapainon johtaja

Erweko Painotuote Oy
Elimäenkatu 17, 00510 Helsinki
Puhelin (90) 718 788
Suora (90) 712 170
Telefax (90) 753 6327

Linda Fu B.GD, AGDA

Principal Design Consultant

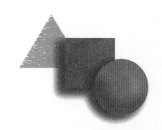

LINDA FU DESIGN

4th Floor State Bank Building
161 London Circuit ACT 2601 Australia
PO Box 828 Civic Square ACT 2608
Telephone: +61 6 248 0823
Facsimile: +61 6 248 0832

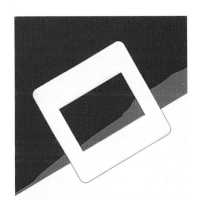

CHRIS O'CONNOR PHOTOGRAPHY

PO Box E297 Queen Victoria Terrace Canberra ACT 2600

MOBILE: 0412 012 701

BASIC, INC.

代表取締役

橋本篤慶

Member of JIDA

株式会社ベイシック
〒559 大阪市住之江区南港北2丁目1-10 ATC,ITM4-N-5
Tel:06-614-3919 Fax:06-615-3033

ARCHITECTS

KBJ Architects, Inc.
510 North Julia Street
Jacksonville, FL 32202
AA C000001
Phone: 904-356-9491
Facsimile: 904-356-1031

1. **NIGEL HOLMES** （USA） Graphic designer グラフィック デザイナー CD, AD, D, I: Nigel Holmes
2. **ERWEKO PAINTOUTE OY** （Finland） Printing 印刷 AD, D: Viktor Kaltala CW: Reijo Taajaranta DF: Viktorno Design Oy
3. **LINDA FU DESIGN** （Australia） Graphic design グラフィック デザイン AD, D, I: Linda Fu DF: Linda Fu Design
4. **CHRIS O'CONNOR PHOTOGRAPHY** （Australia） Photography 写真 AD, D, I: Linda Fu DF: Linda Fu Design
5. **BASIC, INC.** （Japan） Design デザイン D: Hirofumi Akiyama
6. **KBJ ARCHITECTS** （USA） Architecture 建築設計 CD: Tom Schiffanella AD, D: Jefferson Rall D, I: Mike Barnhart DF: Robin Shepherd Studios

1 2 3
4 5 6

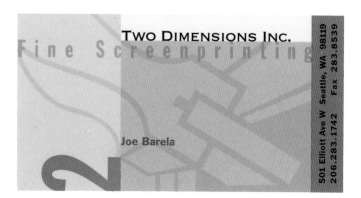

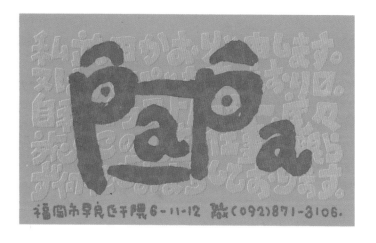

1. **SITE ENVIRONMENTAL DESIGN** （USA） Environmental design 環境デザイン CD, AD, D: Yoshifumi Fujii

2. **SJOQUIST ARCHITECTS INC.** （USA） Architecture 建築設計 CD, AD: John Reger D: Sherwin Schwartzrock DF: Design Center

3. **TWO DIMENSIONS** （USA） Printing 印刷 D: Doug Keyes DF: A / D

4. **ANDREA GRECO DESIGN STUDIO** （USA） Design デザイン AD, D, I: Andrea Greco DF: Andrea Greco Design Studio

5. **PAPA** （Japan） Illustration イラストレーション AD, D: Kaori Takeda DF: Papa

6. **BOB ANDERSON PHOTOGRAPHY** （Canada） Photography 写真 AD: Malcolm Waddell D: Nicola Lyon I: Gary Mansbridge DF: Eskind Wadell

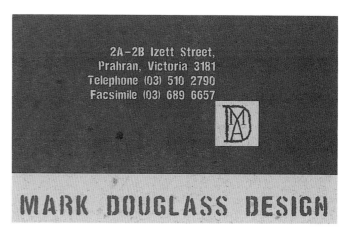

1. **BERGMAN-UNGAR ASSOCIATES** (USA) Advertising 広告 CD, AD, D: Robert Bergman-Ungar DF: Bergman-Ungar Associates

2. **DANIEL FURON** (USA) Photographer 写真家 D: Erik Atigard / Patricia McShane DF: M. A. D.

3. **SANDY GIN DESIGN** (USA) Graphic design グラフィック デザイン D: Sandy Gin DF: Sandy Gin Design

4. **MOI・MÊME** (Japan) Photography 写真 P: Atsumi Yamauchi

5. **FANTASIA DESIGN CO., LTD.** (USA) Graphic design グラフィック デザイン CD, D: Elisa Ling Kuo DF: Fantasia Design Co., Ltd.

6. **MARK DOUGLASS DESIGN** (Australia) Interior design インテリア デザイン AD: Andrew Hoyne D, DF: Andrew Hoyne Design

1 2
3 4
5 6

1. **HIROYUKI TOMINAGA**（Japan）Design デザイン AD, D: Isamu Nakazawa DF: Hi Hat Studio

2. **FUMIO INOUE**（Japan）Graphic designer グラフィック デザイナー AD, D: Fumio Inoue

3. **YUKIKO KIUCHI**（Japan）Illustrator イラストレーター AD, D: Isamu Nakazawa DF: Hi Hat Studio

4. **SHEEHAN DESIGN**（USA）Graphic design グラフィック デザイン CD, AD, D, I: Jamie Sheehan DF: Sheehan Design

5. **ISAMU NAKAZAWA**（Japan）Graphic designer グラフィック デザイナー AD, D: Isamu Nakazawa DF: Hi Hat Studio

6. **ICHIRO HIRAOKA**（Japan）Illustrator イラストレーター AD, D: Isamu Nakazawa DF: Hi Hat Studio

1 2
3 4
5 6

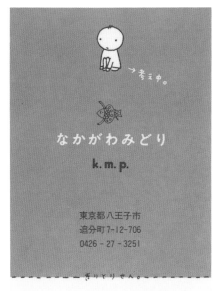

1. **MIDORI NAKAGAWA** （Japan）Designer デザイナー CD, AD, D, I, CW: Midori Nakagawa

2. **HIDETSUGU NISHISAKA** （Japan）Graphic designer グラフィック デザイナー AD, D: Hidetsugu Nishisaka

3. **KATSUMI WANAJO** （Japan）Photographer 写真家 AD: D: Yoshiro Kajitani D: Mayumi Kawabe DF: Kajitani Design Room

4. **STUDIO PEKKA KIIRALA** （Finland）Photography 写真 D: Viktor Kaltala DF: Viktorno Design Oy

5. **SEABROS INC.** （Japan）Design デザイン CD: Masateru Kitada AD, D: Fumihiko Takahara

6. **JOHN NASH & FRIENDS** （UK）Graphic design グラフィック デザイン CD, AD, D: John Nash DF: John Nash & Friends

名 刺

2 3 6 - □ □

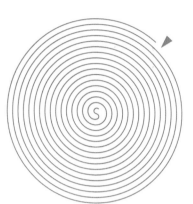

Hiroyuki Miura
Art Director

SLASH inc.

T&A Building, 6-34-17 Jingūmae,
Shibuya-ku, Tokyo 150
Phone 03.3409.4090 Facsimile 03.3409.4033

KEN YOKOGAWA ARCHITECT & ASSOCIATES INC.

プロジェクト主査
所長代理
宿本和則

株式会社 横河設計工房
〒106 東京都港区西麻布4-18-9
アーバンコートB1
Telephone:03-3486-4116
Facsimile:03-3486-4056

企画・編集・原稿執筆
黒原康一郎

電話：〇四五-七八六-二二六〇
電送：〇四五-七八六-三九八七
ニフティーID：JAF〇三三五七

神奈川県横浜市金沢区
釜利谷東6丁目34-1-517

CHIEF DESIGNER
横井祐子

有限会社イデアポリス

〒461 名古屋市東区代官町16番17号 三愛ビル2・10F
TEL 052・933・0252 FAX 052・937・4322

VALE
crear
una
obra

Graphic Designer
YU TA KA SA SA KI

#301, KAWAGUCHIYA, BLDG.
4-72 SUEYOSHI-CHO, NAKA-KU,
YOKOHAMA, 231 JAPAN
TEL. 045-263-0436 FAX. 045-263-0436

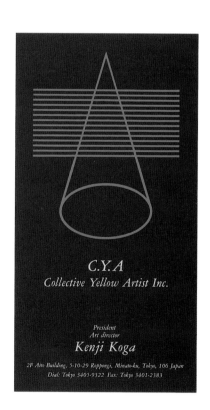

C.Y.A
Collective Yellow Artist Inc.

President
Art director
Kenji Koga

2F Aito Building, 5-10-29 Roppongi, Minato-ku, Tokyo, 106 Japan
Dial: Tokyo 3405-9322 Fax: Tokyo 3401-2383

1. **SLASH INC.** （Japan）Advertising 広告 AD, D, DF: Slash Inc.

2. **KOICHIRO KUROHARA** （Japan）Writer ライター AD, D: Yoshihiro Madachi DF: Design Studio Waters

3. **IDEAPOLIS** （Japan）Advertising 広告 CD: Yoshie Yoshida D: Yuko Yokoi DF: Ideapolis

4. **KEN YOKOGAWA ARCHITECT & ASSOCIATES INC.** （Japan）Architecture 建築設計 AD: Masaaki Hiromura D: Nobuhiko Aizawa DF: Hiromura Design Office

5. **CREAR UNA OBRA VALE!** （Japan）Graphic design グラフィック デザイン CD, AD: Yutaka Sasaki D: Kaori Yanagisawa DF: Crear Una Obra Vale!

6. **COLLECTIVE YELLOW ARTIST INC.** （Japan）Design デザイン AD: Kenji Koga

1 2 3

4 5 6

C O R B I S

Corbis Publishing

15395
SE 30th Place
Suite 300
Bellevue
Washington
98007

206/649-3369

curtisw@corbis.com
curtiswong@aol.com

Curtis Wong
Executive Producer

Fax 206/746-1618

海光印刷有限公司
HOI KWONG PRINTING CO, LTD

香港鰂魚涌船塢里八號華廈工業大廈六樓C－D座
5/F Block C–D, Wah Ha Industry Building
8 Shipyard Lane, Quarry Bay, Hong Kong
Tel: 562 1096   562 1641   Fax: 564 2142

Finished Art inc.

Donna Johnston

708 Antone St. N.W. Atlanta, Ga 30318
Phone ‹404› 355-7902   Fax ‹404› 352-3846

Włodzimierz SKONIECZKA

GRAFIKA   Zakład Wydawniczo - Poligraficzny

ul. Przędzalniana 20
90 - 034 Łódź
tel./ fax (0 42) 74 41 99
tlx 884423

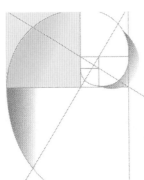

Thomas E. Duke • Architect

Architecture, Space Planning, Design
1807 University Boulevard South
Jacksonville • Florida 32216
904 • 721-0434 • Fax 904 • 721-0835

Thomas E. Duke, AIA, NCARB
Lic. #AR0013266 • NCARB 53,097

Tony Trobe   Architect BA(Arch), B(Arch), ARAIA

TT ARCHITECTURE

6 Monaghan Place NICHOLLS ACT 2913

Telephone (06) 242 8622 Facsimile (06) 242 8620

1. **CORBIS** (USA) Publisher 出版 AD, D: Jack Anderson D: John Anicker / David Bates DF: Hornall Anderson Design Works, Inc.
2. **HOI KWONG PRINTING CO., LTD.** (Hong Kong) Printing 印刷
  CD: Kan Tai-keung AD, D: Clement Yick Tat Wa D: Eric Cheung DF: Kan Tai-keung Design & Associates Ltd.
3. **FINISHED ART INC.** (USA) Graphic design グラフィック デザイン AD: Donna Johnston D: Kannex Fung DF: Finished Art Inc.
4. **GRAFIKA** (Poland) Publisher 出版 CD, AD, D: Tadeusz Piechura CW: Wlodzimierz Skonieczka DF: Atelier Tadeusz Piechura
5. **THOMAS E. DUKE** (USA) Architecture 建築設計 AD, D, I: Chris Smith DF: Robin Shepherd Studios
6. **TT ARCHITECTURE** (Australia) Architecture 建築設計 AD, D: Linda Fu DF: Linda Fu Design

1 2
3 4
5 6

1. **YOKO YOSHIDA** （Japan） Illustrator　イラストレーター　AD, D: Masaru Yoshida

2. **YOSHINO DESIGN OFFICE INC.** （Japan） Graphic design　グラフィック デザイン　AD: Shuhei Yoshino　D: Hisako Chatani

3. **KOCHI HAJIME** （Japan） Illustrator　イラストレーター　AD, I: Kochi Hajime

4. **LESLIE CHAN DESIGN CO., LTD.** （Taiwan） Graphic design　グラフィック デザイン　CD, AD, D: Chan Wing Kei, Leslie　DF: Leslie Chan Design Co., Ltd.

C
H
I
E

鷹有人
（荒川タカユキ）
郵便番号二四八
鎌倉市七里ヶ浜東
五丁目十一番三号
（湘南分室）
電話・ファックス
〇四六七-三三-一四七三

(takayuki arakawa)
5-11-3
seven miles beach east,
kamakura-city,
kanagawa 248 japan
phone & fax:
0467-33-1473

黒田亜紀

映像本舗
竜屋亜喜助
616京都市右京区
太秦安井馬塚町
18の1 電話075
841 5455 電送
075 841 5466

土井千恵

イキ
消し誤りそのまま
でよし
連続させよ
一字あけよ
字間をつめよ
新らしく行を起せ
横字、倒字を直せ
良い活字と坂かへよ
文字の位置を置きかへよ
上げよ
下げよ
右に移せ
左に移せ
取り去れ

代表
吉田外次郎

タイポグラフィス／小金哲志
〒151 東京都渋谷区上原2-29-8 Yu-Flats 5B T:03-3469-2320 F:03-3469-2321

1. **TAKAYUKI ARAKAWA** （Japan） Critic 評論家 AD, D: Masaru Yoshida
2. **TATSUYA AKISUKE** （Japan） Film production 映像制作 AD, D: Isamu Nakazawa DF: Hi Hat Studio
3. **CHIE DOI** （Japan） Copywriter コピーライター D: Akihiko Tsukamoto
4. **YAMATO INC.** （Japan） Printing 印刷 D: Akihiko Tsukamoto
5. **TYPOGRAPHIS** （Japan） Typography タイポグラフィー AD, D, I: Tetsushi Kokin DF: Typographis

1 2 3
4 5

Tom H. Raatz

Lighting Specialist

BECKLEY IMPORTS INC.

209 16TH STREET

DES MOINES, IOWA 50309

(515) 243-8185

FAX 243-8712

BOSCH AUTHORIZED SERVICE

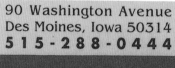

90 Washington Avenue
Des Moines, Iowa 50314
515-288-0444

Polite Design

Kerry Polite

Graphic Design

Twenty One Sixteen
Locust Street

Philadelphia,
Pennsylvania 19103

Telephone
{215} 985.4818

Facsimile
{215} 985.9402

STEVE BECKLEY

**EUROPEAN
CAR SERVICE**

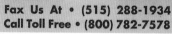

Fax Us At • (515) 288-1934
Call Toll Free • (800) 782-7578

1. **BECKLEY IMPORTS** （USA） Auto repairs 自動車修理 CD, AD, D, I: John Sayles DF: Sayles Graphic Design
2. **ADVENTURE LIGHTING** （USA） Lighting consultant 照明コンサルタント CD, AD, D, I: John Sayles DF: Sayles Graphic Design
3. **POLITE DESIGN** （USA） Designer デザイナー D: Kerry Polite DF: Polite Design

1
2
3

100

Douglas Jones

Program Director

BAY 2 BAY
USA

4390 Valeta St.

San Diego, CA

Zip Code 92107

Tel. 619 226 8888

INTERNATIONAL PRINTING CENTER

YOUNG DON JOO
Vice President International Operations

CORPORATE OFFICE
3530 EAST 28TH STREET
MINNEAPOLIS, MN 55406
612.722.0472 FAX 612.721.6303

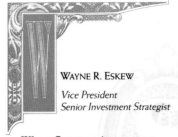

WAYNE R. ESKEW

Vice President
Senior Investment Strategist

WALL STREET ADVISORS

950 Interchange Tower

600 South Hwy 169

Minneapolis, Mn 55426

Pho 612-546-5657

800-359-6078

Fax 612-546-5672

Ken Leggio

Global Marketing, Limited

2040 Fairway Circle, NE

Atlanta, Georgia 30319

Phone 404.634.5136

Facsimile 404.329.0932

Maureen McManus

MANAGER
◇
LINN HOUSE
KEITH
BANFFSHIRE AB55 3BU
SCOTLAND
TELEPHONE
01542 783450
FACSIMILE
01542 783451

Rob

Walker

375 Walsh Road

Atherton, California 94026

415-854-1139 Fax 415-854-1889

1. **PENINSULA FAMILY YMCA** （USA） Family recreation リクリエーション センター CD, AD, D: José Serrano DF: Mires Design, Inc.
2. **INTERNATIONAL PRINTING CENTER** （USA） Printing broker 印刷仲買 CD, AD: John Reger D: Kobe DF: Design Center
3. **WALL STREET ADVISORS** （USA） Financial consultants 財務コンサルタント CD, AD: John Reger D: Todd Spichke DF: Design Center
4. **GLOBAL MARKETING** （USA） Marketing consultant マーケティング コンサルタント CD: Pattie Belle Hastings AD, D: Bjorn Akselsen DF: Icehouse Design
5. **THE CHIVAS & GLENLIVET GROUP** （UK） Whisky supplier ウィスキー会社 CD, AD, D: John Nash I: John Lawrence DF: John Nash & Friends
6. **ROB WALKER** （USA） Business consultant ビジネス コンサルタント CD, AD: Lawrence Bender D: Margaret Hellmann DF: Lawrence Bender & Associates

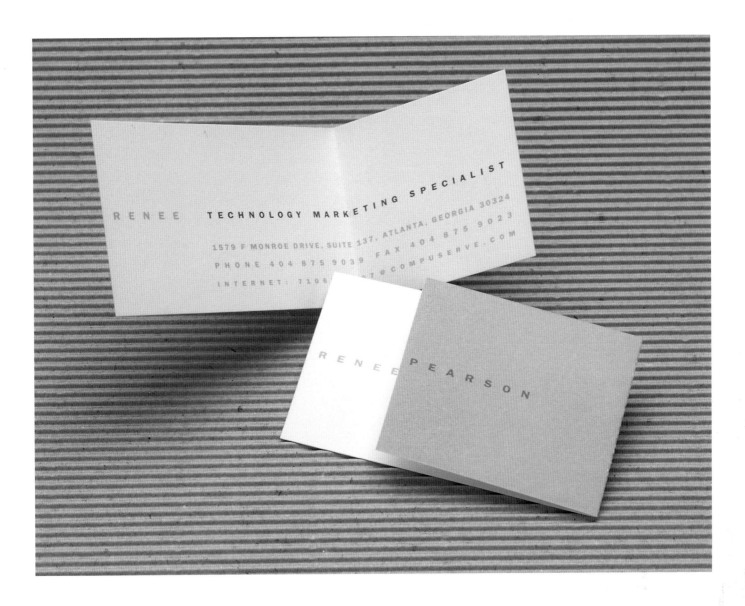

OPPOSITE PAGE: **MIKE McCONNELL** （USA） Fitness trainer フィットネス トレーナー D, I: Doug Keyes DF: A / D

1. **RENEE PEARSON** （USA） Consulting コンサルティング CD: Pattie Belle Hastings AD, D: Bjorn Akselsen DF: Icehouse Design

2. **PROFIT RETENTION CONCEPTS** （USA） Consulting コンサルティング AD, D: Mark Silvers DF: Melia Design Group

3. **SPICERS PAPER** （Australia） Paper merchant 紙業者 AD, D: Andrew Hoyne D: Amanda McPherson DF: Andrew Hoyne Design

1

2 3

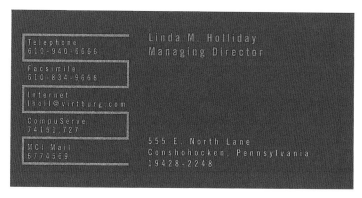

1. **RF** （Netherlands） Event planning イベント企画 CD, AD, D, DF: Limage Dangereuse

2. **THE KILGANNON GROUP** （USA） Direct response agency ダイレクト リスポンス CD, AD, D: Steve Rousso DF: Rousso + Associates

3. **CURRENT COMMUNICATIONS COMPANY** （USA） Health education ヘルス ケア D: Kerry Polite DF: Polite Design

1
2
3

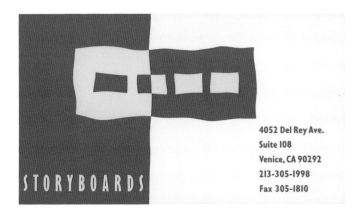

1. **YAMAMOTO DENTIST** （Japan） Dentist **歯科医** AD, D: Masako Ban
2. **IMPRESS HEINEN & FRANKEN** （Germany） Public relations **宣伝** CD, D: Detlef Behr DF: Büro für Kommunikationsdesign
3. **JENNIFER MORRISON** （USA） Storyboard artist **ストーリーボード** CD, AD: Petrula Vrontikis D: Bob Dinetz DF: Vrontikis Design Office
4. **SELECT ONE** （USA） Computer consultant **コンピューター コンサルタント** CD, AD: Richard Seireeni D: James Pezzullo DF: Studio Seireeni
5. **ANDREW M. LAURIA** （USA） Real estate **不動産** CD, AD: Petrula Vrontikis D: Kim Sage DF: Vrontikis Design Office

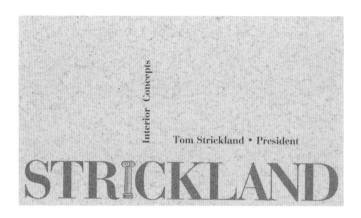

1035 May Street
Jacksonville, Florida 32204
Telephone (904) 353-9123

1. **TOM STRICKLAND INTERIORS** （USA）Interior consultant インテリア コンサルタント
CD, AD, D: Jefferson Rall CD: Tom Schiffanella I: Mike Barnhart DF: Robin Shepherd Studios
2. **RITA'S CATERING & EVENT PLANNING** （USA）Catering ケータリング CD, D: Mark Oldach DF: Mark Oldach Design, Ltd.
3. **OCCASIONAL OCCASIONS** （USA）Catering ケータリング CD: Marcia Romanuck D: Fran McKay I: Clip Art DF: The Design Company
4. **PONTE VEDRA ESTATES** （USA）Real estate 不動産 CD, AD, D: David Brent Lee DF: Robin Shepherd Studios

1
2
3 4

GREG COLEMAN
Director of Marketing
Tel. 612.339.5218

RETIREMENT AND ESTATE ADVISORS

1320 Metropolitan Centre   Minneapolis, Minnesota   Fax 612. 337.5070
333 South 7th Street   Zip 55402

MIDCOM   MIDCOM TOWER   TEL 206.628.8422

COMMUNICATIONS   1111 THIRD AVENUE   FAX 206.628.8171

INC.   SEATTLE, WA 98101

MICHELE M. JOHNSON

Human Resources Specialist

1. **RETIREMENT AND ESTATE ADVISORS** （USA) Financial consultants 財務コンサルタント CD, AD: John Reger D: Sherwin Schwartzrock DF: Design Center

2. **MIDCOM COMMUNICATIONS** （USA) Phone line dealer 電話回線ディーラー AD, D: John Hornall D: Jana Nishi DF: Hornall Anderson Design Works

3. **SHADES SALON** （Canada) Hair and make-up salon ヘアメーク サロン AD, D, I: Catharine Bradbury DF: Bradbury Design Inc.

FILTER

Consultancy
voor jong creatief
en strategisch talent

Tineke
Hey

Ter Kleef 15
1081 AM Amsterdam

Tel: 020-6448503
Fax: 020-4040094

ACTOR
212.978.0841

Kelly Sue DeConnick

creative
spunky
confident
funky

anita burger
hair & make up

1. **FILTER** (Netherlands) Talent scout タレント スカウト CD, D: Ron Van Der Vlugt D: Rob Verhaart DF: Designers Company
2. **KELLY SUE DECONNICK** (USA) Actor 俳優 CD, D, I: Patty J. Palazzo AD: Molly J. Zakrajsek DF: Triple Seven Design
3. **ANITA BURGER** (UK) Stylist スタイリスト CD, AD, D: Hermann Brändle CD, AD, D: Sigi Ramoser DF: Atelier für Text und Gestaltung

1. **KAZUYA KUSUYAMA** （Japan） Hair and make-up artist ヘアメーク アーティスト D: Kazuki DF: Tyrell Studio

2. **ATOMIC GARDEN TATTOOS** （USA） Tattoo studio タトゥー スタジオ CD, AD, D: Adrianna Jumping Eagle I: Gilbert Jumping Eagle DF: Jumping Eagle Design

3. **MR. REYNOLDS LIMOUSINE** （USA） Limousine service リムジン サービス CD, AD, D, I: John Sayles DF: Sayles Graphic Design

4. **COMPU CAMPUS** （USA） Computer college コンピューター専門学校 CD, AD, D, I: Jack Tom DF: Jack Tom Design

5. **MAKOTO YOSHIDA** （Japan） Musician ミュージシャン AD, D: Masaru Yoshida

TOM EGGUM

C O M M U N I C A T I O N S

Tom Eggum Speaker/Author

P.O. Box 5268 • Glendale, Arizona 85312 • (602) 978-1719

MEDIKO**DENTAL**

Dr. **Adnan ÜNSAL**, Genel Müdür

Merkez: Kuleli sok. 1/6 G.O.P. 06700 Ankara.
tel: (312) 437 78 51 fax: 436 29 74
Klinik: Kazakistan cad. (4. Cad.) 71. sok. 5/3
Emek 06510 Ankara. tel: (312) 221 34 44

FOCUS

COMMUNICATIONS

2-9 MASONS AVENUE
LONDON EC2V 5BT
TELEPHONE 071-600 1392
FAX 071-600 1365

Daniel D. Pearson

Focus Communications Group is a financial and international corporate communications consultancy, working with public and private companies, professional practices and financial institutions. We aim to improve the bottom line performance of our clients through a proven combination of communication skills and marketing techniques.

Ray Olguin, R.T.
Consultant of X-Ray Products

348 West Turney
Phoenix, AZ 85013
602/279-3751

Office

PINNACLE ALLIANCE
Achieving Excellence Through
Global Partnership

Thomas R. Madison
Computer Sciences Corporation
3160 Fairview Park Drive
Falls Church, Virginia 22042
703.876.1228

1. **TOM EGGUM COMMUNICATIONS** （USA） Motivational speaker 演説家 CD, AD, D: Greg Walters DF: Greg Walters Design
2. **MEDIKODENTAL LTD.** （France） Dentist 歯科医 D: Koray Ozgen / Beril Edguer Ozgen DF: Ozgen
3. **FOCUS COMMUNICATION** （UK） Corporate communications consultant コミュニケーション コンサルタント CD, AD, D: John Nash DF: John Nash & Friends
4. **RAY OLGUIN** （USA） Medical equipment consultant 医療機器コンサルタント CD, AD, D: Al Luna P: Ray Olguin DF: Luna Design
5. **COMPUTER SCIENCES CORPORATION** （USA） Consulting コンサルティング
CD: Mary Jo Ordreijka AD, D: Ramonn Hutko P: Gnass DF: Computer Sciences Corporation

1 2
3
4 5

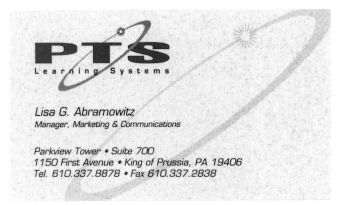

1. **PRO SHOP BIG** （Japan） Dry cleaning クリーニング D: Yutaka Yoshida DF: Matrix

2. **PTS LEARNING SYSTEMS** （USA） Computer trainer コンピューター トレーナー CD: Jerry Selber AD, D, I: Wicky W. Lee DF: Kaiser Feinberg & Associates Inc.

3. **LANDERER & COMPANY** （Australia） Law practice 弁護士 CD: Tony Masters AD, D, I: Carol Whittaker P: Willem Rethmeier DF: Tony Masters Design

4. **RISK MANAGEMENT GROUP** （USA） Investment 投資家 CD, AD, D: James Picquelle DF: Aloha Printing

5. **FULL ARTS METAL WORKS LTD.** （Hong Kong） Curtain wall tailoring カーテンウォール テイラー
CD: Kan Tai-keung AD, D: Clement Yick Tat Wa D: Janny Lee Yin Wa DF: Kan Tai-keung Design & Associates Ltd.

1 2
3
4 5

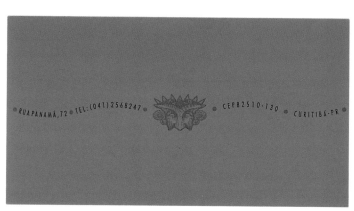

Karen McDonald

Practice Consultant

Mercy Healthcare San Diego
3900 Fifth Avenue, #310
San Diego, CA 92103
(619) 543-8150
Fax (619) 291-2678

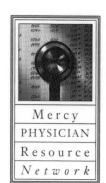

1. **OASIS** （USA） Book keeping 簿記 AD, D: Janél Apple DF: Kowalski Designworks, Inc.

2. **LAUREL ENGEL** （USA） Landscape designer 景観デザイナー AD, D: Krysten Bonzelet DF: Kowalski Designworks, Inc.

3. **BASTIDORES** （Brazil） Costume production 衣装制作 CD, AD: Silvio Silva Junior CD: Mirian Hatori D: Karine Mitsue Kawamura DF: Studio Lumen Design

4. **MERCY HEALTHCARE - SAN DIEGO** （USA） Hospital 病院 CD, AD, D: John Ball DF: Mires Design, Inc.

5. **SUSAN GAGE CATERING** （USA） Catering ケータリング AD, D: Samuel G. Shelton DF: Kinetik Communication Graphics, Inc.

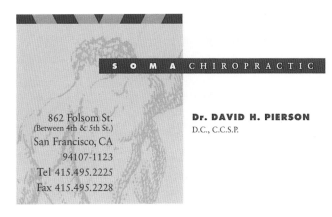

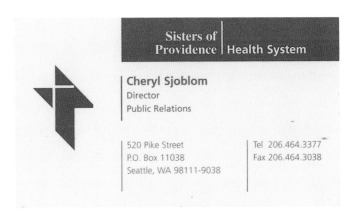

1. **MOORE & ASSOCIATES** （USA） Consulting コンサルティング CD, AD, D: Scott Mires D: Deborah Fukushima DF: Mires Design, Inc.

2. **SOMA CHIROPRACTIC** （USA） Chiropractic カイロプラクティック
CD, AD, D: Mark Sackett D: Wayne Sakamoto / James Sakamoto DF: Sackett Design Associates

3. **GLOBAL ACCESS INC.** （USA） Telecommunication service 通信サービス CD, AD: John Reger D: Sherwin Schwartzrock DF: Design Center

4. **FRANCISCAN HEALTH SYSTEM** （USA） Health care ヘルス ケア CD, AD: Rick Eiber D: Giorgio Davanzo DF: Rick Eiber Design

5. **SISTERS OF PROVIDENCE** （USA） Health care ヘルス ケア CD, AD: Rick Eiber D: David Balzer DF: Rick Eiber Design

6. **D. A. R. T.** （Germany） Cycle services 自転車サービス CD, AD, D, I, CW: Udo Würth DF: Faktor, Design & Funktion

1 2
3 4
5 6

QUEBECOR
INTEGRATED MEDIA

BRIAN F. DAMMEIER
Vice-Chairman of the Board

P.O. Box 1418, Tacoma, WA 98401
800.451.5742 206.922.9393
Fax: 206.922.3383

Turning
Technology
Into
Solutions

QUEBECOR
INTEGRATED M

BRIAN F. DAMMEIER
Vice-Chairman of the Board

P.O. Box 1418, Tacoma, WA 98401
800.451.5742 206.922.939
Fax: 206.922.3383

Turning
Technology
Into
Solutions

QUE
IN

Turning
Technology
Into
Solutions

BRIAN F. DAMMEI
Vice-Chairman of the B
P.O. Box 1418, Tacoma, WA
800.451.5742 206.922.9393
Fax: 6.922.3383

Plant Address:
4918 20th Street East
Fife, WA 98424

ELAINE ARONIS

MARKETING DIRECTOR

M O T O R
W O R K S
BY AUTOCRAFT

1116 EAST DOUGLAS

WICHITA, KS 67214

TEL 316 267-8888

FAX 316 265-0766

SPECIALIZING IN

HONDA MAZDA NISSAN TOYOTA

Mag. Michael
Rubak

Wirtschafts-
treuhänder
Steuerberater

1180 Wien
Hofstattgasse 13

T 470 65 63
F 470 65 63-19

03(3223)4624 telefon

tomo@media

4 1 12 308

杉山知之

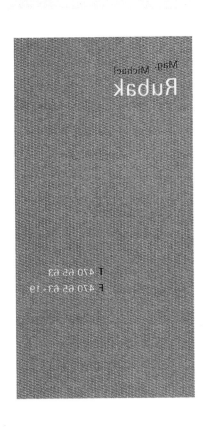

tomoyuki sugiyama

.cst.nihon-u.ac.jp

杉並区高円寺北

post 166

OPPOSITE PAGE: **QUEBECOR** (USA) Turn-key services ターンキー サービス
AD, D: Jack Anderson D: Heidi Favour / Mary Hermes / Mary Chin Hutchison D, I: Julia LaPine DF: Hornall Anderson Design Works, Inc.

1. **MOTORWORKS** (USA) Auto repairs 自動車修理 CD, AD, D: Sonia Greteman D: James Strange DF: Greteman Group

2. **TREUMANDAT GMBH** (Austria) Tax accountant 税理士 CD, AD, D: Clemens Heider DF: Atelier Heider

3. **TOMOYUKI SUGIYAMA** (Japan) Multimedia consultant メディア コンサルタント AD, D: Takeshi Maeda

1
2
3

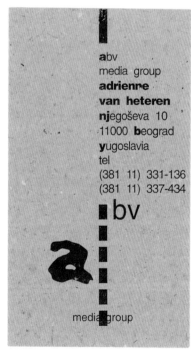

1. **MEIWA KIM** （Japan）Flower stylist **フラワー スタイリスト** AD, D: Isamu Nakazawa DF: Hi Hat Studio

2. **ABV** （Netherlands）Media organization **メディア協会** CD, AD, D, CW: Škart DF: Škart Group

3. **CLOUDBREAK MGMT.** （USA）Artist management **アーティスト マネージメント** CD, AD, D: Ellie Leacock DF: Art Stuff

1

2 3

ANNIE MEACHAM

515-282-7080

515 28th Street Suite 106A
Des Moines, Iowa   50312
515-282-7080   Fax 243-3460

Sheila Hughes
Public Relations Director
Phone (206) 622-5123 ext. 6928
Fax (206) 622-5154

BUMBERSHOOT 95
The Seattle Arts Festival
25th anniversary

One Reel P.O. Box 9750 Seattle, WA 98109-0750

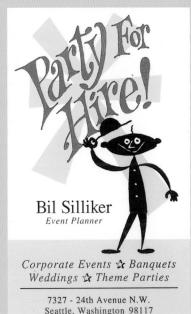

Party For Hire!

Bil Silliker
Event Planner

Corporate Events ☆ Banquets
Weddings ☆ Theme Parties

7327 - 24th Avenue N.W.
Seattle, Washington 98117
Partyline ☞ (206) **782-4802**

1. **A. MEACHAM CREATIVE** （USA） Consulting **コンサルティング** CD, AD, D, I: John Sayles DF: Sayles Graphic Design
2. **ONE REEL** （USA） Event planner **イベント企画** CD, AD, D, I: Robynne Raye DF: Modern Dog
3. **BIL SILLIKER** （USA） Event planner **イベント企画** CD, AD, D, I, CW: Michael Strassburger DF: Modern Dog

1

2 3

1. **RIVE GANSHE**　（Japan）　Hair salon　ヘア サロン　CD, AD, D: Hisako Asai　DF: Design Studio Mint

2. **WADE RIPKA**　（USA）　Composer　作曲家　CD, AD, D: Robert Padovano　DF: Robert Padovano Design

3. **THE VILLAGE**　（USA）　Recording studio　レコーディング スタジオ
CD, AD: Mike Salisbury　D: Mary Evelyn McGough　I: Rafael Peixoto Ferrira　DF: Mike Salisbury Communications

1　2

3

DENNIS
HAYES
&
associates
incorporated

305 East 46 Street New York NY 10017-3058
telephone 212 980 0300 fax 212 755 1737

Prof. Dieter Hamann
Dipl.-Ing.

Fachbereich 08
Mathematik
Naturwissenschaften
Datenverarbeitung

Igelweg 48
D-65428 Rüsselsheim
Telefon 06142-65739

Am Brückweg 26
D-65428 Rüsselsheim
Telefon 06142-898-422
Telefax 06142-898-421

Fachhochschule Wiesbaden

ARCH ASSET MANAGEMENT

MARY M. PETERSON, CFP
(612) 893-9805

3300 EDINBOROUGH WAY, EDINA, MINNESOTA 55435 SUITE 500
A REGISTERED INVESTMENT ADVISORY FIRM

1. **DENNIS HAYES** （USA） Video editing ビデオ編集 CD, AD: Stefan Sagmeister D: Eric Zim DF: Sagmeister Inc.

2. **FACHHOCHSCHULE WIESBADEN** （Germany） College 大学 CD, AD, D, I: Doris Jausly / Claudia Ochsenbauer DF: D'sign & Co

3. **ARCH ASSET MANAGEMENT** （USA） Financial investment 財務投資 CD, AD: John Reger D: Dan Olson DF: Design Center

1
2
3

1. **COMMUNITY PARTNERSHIP OF SANTA CLARA COUNTY** (USA) Non-profit organization 慈善団体 CD, AD, D, I: Fani Chung DF: Gee + Chung Design

2. **TWO WEEKS BARBER SHOP** (USA) Barber 理髪店 D: Doug Keyes DF: A / D

3. **JULIE CASCIOPPO** (USA) Vocalist ボーカリスト D: Giorgio Davanzo DF: Giorgio Davanzo Design

Radio Gabby

936 Twenty-First Street
Santa Monica CA 90403
(310) 453.7615

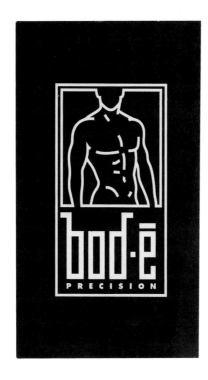

bod-ē
PRECISION

Jill's

CLEANSWEEP

JILL ENGELHART
542·4097

LICENSED HOUSECLEANING

food

S u e   W h i t e
218 Forbes Avenue
San Rafael, CA 94901
4 1 5 . 4 5 9 . 5 0 4 1

PRECISION

PERSONAL

TRAINING

JOHN   PIÑA

619.490.0504

BOONSHOFT
VINTAGE RENTALS

Vintage RENTALS

270 LAFAYETTE ST. #904
NEW YORK NEW YORK 10012
(212) 582-8800
— 24 HOUR SERVICE NUMBER —

NEVE·FAIRCHILD·PULTEC
API·LANG·TUBETECH AND MORE...

1. **RADIO GABBY** （USA） Fitness trainer フィットネス トレーナー CD, AD: Stan Evenson D: Glenn Sakamoto DF: Evenson Design Group
2. **JOHN PINA** （USA） Fitness trainer フィットネス トレーナー CD: José Serrano AD ,D, I: Mike Brower I: Miguel Perez DF: Mires Design, Inc.
3. **JILL'S CLEANSWEEP** （USA） House cleaning 清掃会社 CD, AD, D: Greg Walters DF: Greg Walters Design
4. **SUE WHITE** （USA） Food stylist フード スタイリスト CD: Traci Shiro AD, D, I: Richard Shiro DF: A Small Ad Shop
5. **DAVE BOONSHOFT** （USA） Rentals レンタル CD, AD, I: Stefan Sagmeister D: Veronica Oh DF: Sagmeister Inc.

1 2 3

4 5

VAZARA basic
Hair & Make-up Salon

上原 ヒロ子

Hiroko Uehara

渋谷区元代々木町 2-9 シティハウス代々木公園 2F 〒151
2F Cityhouse Yoyogikoen, 2-9 Motoyoyogi-cho, Shibuya-ku,
Tokyo, 151 Japan Tel.5454-4117 Fax.5454-4137

Daddy
Paddy
Buddy

ダディ・パディ・バディ

インテリアコーディネーター

咲 本 洋 子

ＩＳＩＤ会員
(国際インテリアデザイナー協会)

〒106 港区南麻布4-5-66
ＴＥＬ03・5423・5375
ＦＡＸ03・3444・6672

Hair & Make-up Artists
2F Cityhouse Yoyogikoen
2-9 Motoyoyogi-cho, Shi
buya-ku, Tokyo, 151 Japan
Telephone. 03-5454-4136
Facsimile. 03-5454-4137

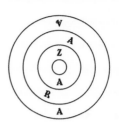

依田 豊
Yutaka Yoda
〒151 渋谷区元代々木町2-9
シティハウス代々木公園 2F
Tel.03-5454-4136
Fax.03-5454-4137

Writer
上田 有紀
Yuki Ueda

Office
mercy

〒232 神奈川県横浜市
南区中村町5-319-3
ワコーレ吉野町ガーデン214

TEL・FAX **045-253-3701**

5-319-3-214 Nakamura-cho
Minami-ku Yokohama-city
Kanagawa, Japan ZIP.232
Tel·Fax 045-253-3701

◎FFICE ◎NE

安 藤 登志男

HEAD OFFICE
〒462 名古屋市北区安井4-9-7
TEL 052・911・2429 FAX 052・911・2435

DESIGN OFFICE IDEAPOLIS
TEL 052・933・0252 FAX 052・937・4322

giampiero enderli

dr med fmh psichiatria
e psicoterapia

via pioda 15
6600 locarno

telefono
093 32 26 41

natel
077 86 95 00

telefax
093 32 26 43

1. **VAZARA BASIC** （*Japan*） Hair salon ヘアサロン AD, D: Yoshiro Kajitani D: Michiko Arakawa DF: Kajitani Design Room
2. **DADDY PADDY BUDDY** （*Japan*） Interior coordinator インテリア コーディネーター AD, D: Hiroshi Morishima DF: Time-space-art Inc.
3. **VAZARA** （*Japan*） Hair and make-up artist ヘアメーク アーティスト CD: Kenji Hanaue AD: D: Yoshiro Kajitani DF: Kajitani Design Room
4. **OFFICE MERCY** （*Japan*） Writer ライター CD, AD, D: Mika Yaida DF: Mowe Design Office
5. **OFFICE ONE** （*Japan*） Office fitting オフィス内装 D: Yuko Yokoi DF: Ideapolis
6. **GIAMPIERO ENDERLI** （*Switzerland*） Psychiatrist 精神科医 CD, AD, D: Oberholzer Tagli Knobel

1 2 3
4 5 6

1. **YOUNG IMAGINATIONS** （USA）Arts education 芸術教育 CD, AD, D: Mark Sackett I: Wayne Sakamoto DF: Sackett Design Associates
2. **MAI GOTO** （Japan）Producer プロデューサー D: Akihiko Tsukamoto
3. **INTERNATIONAL MEDIA RESEARCH FOUNDATION** （Japan）Media research メディア リサーチ AD, D: Takeshi Maeda
4. **UMWELTINFORMATIONSDIENST VORARLBERG** （Austria）Information service 情報サービス CD, AD, D, I: Sigi Ramoser

1 2 3
4

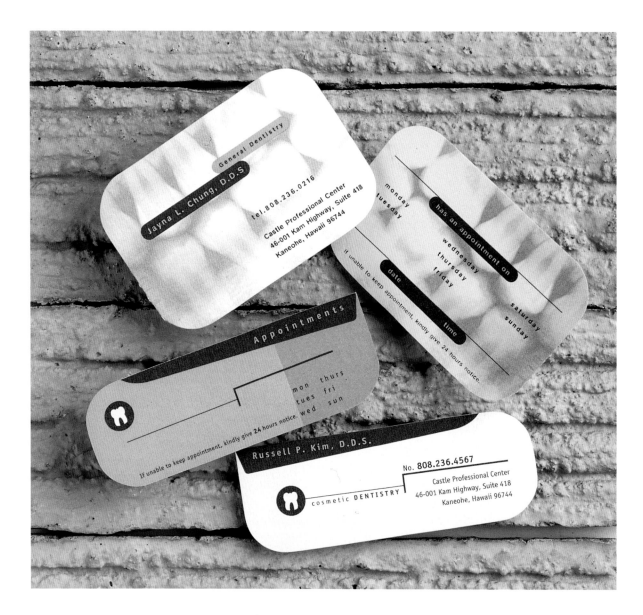

Daissy Farias
MASSAGE & REIKI
415.458.9703

1. **DR. JAYNA L. CHUNG** （USA） Dentist 歯科医 AD, D: Rhonda Kim DF: Rhonda Kim Design
2. **DR. RUSSEL P. KIM** （USA） Dentist 歯科医 AD, D: Rhonda Kim DF: Rhonda Kim Design
3. **EL ROTRINGO** （France） Performer パフォーマー CD, AD, D: Jean-Jacques Tachdjian DF: I Comme Image
4. **DAISSY FARIAS** （USA） Massage therapist マッサージ師 D: Erik Atigard / Patricia Mcshane DF: M. A. D.

1
2
3 4

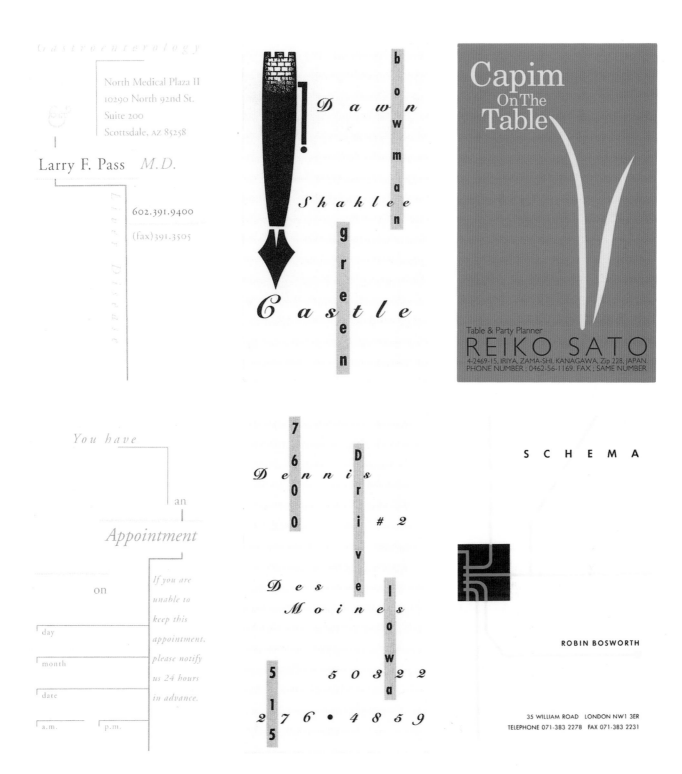

Gastroenterology

North Medical Plaza II
10290 North 92nd St.
Suite 200
Scottsdale, AZ 85258

Larry F. Pass *M.D.*

602.391.9400

(fax)391.3505

Dawn

Shaklee

bowman

green

Castle

Capim
On The
Table

Table & Party Planner
REIKO SATO
4-2469-15, IRIYA, ZAMA-SHI, KANAGAWA, Zip 228, JAPAN.
PHONE NUMBER : 0462-56-1169. FAX : SAME NUMBER

You have

an

Appointment

on

day

month

date

a.m.   p.m.

If you are
unable to
keep this
appointment,
please notify
us 24 hours
in advance.

Dennis

7600

Des
Moines

Drive

#2

Iowa

5
1
5

5 0 3 2 2

2 7 6 • 4 8 5 9

S C H E M A

ROBIN BOSWORTH

35 WILLIAM ROAD   LONDON NW1 3ER
TELEPHONE 071-383 2278   FAX 071-383 2231

1. **LARRY F. PASS** (USA) Physician 医師 D: Elaine Lokelani Lum-King DF: Skolos / Wedell, Inc.

2. **CASTLE GREEN** (USA) Writer ライター CD, AD, D, I: John Sayles DF: Sayles Graphic Design

3. **CAPIM ON THE TABLE** （Japan) Tableware coordinator テーブル コーディネーター AD, D: Yoshihiro Madachi DF: Design Studio Waters

4. **SCHEMA** （UK) Computer services コンピューター サービス CD: John Nash AD, D: Peta Miller DF: John Nash & Friends

PROJETOS E ILUMINAÇÃO **DOMINICI**

LEILA DE MIRANDA SABOIA

ILLUMINARE PROJETOS E ILUMINAÇÃO LTDA.
RUA BENJAMIN LINS (AV. BATEL),779
TEL./FAX: (55-041)234 3999
CEP 80420-100 CURITIBA PARANÁ BRASIL

▶ Simone Geiger

EVERGREEN

GARTEN- UND LANDSCHAFTSBAU
THOMAS FISCHER

▶ Kaiser-Karl-Ring 38c ▶ 53111 Bonn
▶ Fon 02 28-68 01 23 ▶ Fax 02 28-67 98 11

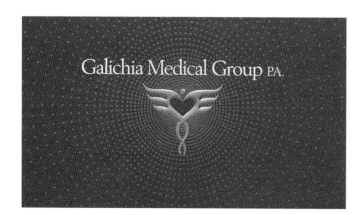

Galichia Medical Group P.A.

Care that Starts from the Heart

Health Strategies Plaza
551 N. Hillside, Suite 410
Post Office Box 47668
Wichita, KS 67201-7668

Doug Kaufman
Associate Administrator

Telephone 316-684-3838
Toll Free 1-800-657-7250
Facsimile 316-688-9183

internet
providers
rotterdam

ROLAND ROTHENHÖFER
william boothlaan 19a
3012 vh rotterdam
tel 010 4330176
fax 010 412 67 38

e-mail: ROLAND @ ipr. NL

DIENST
stedelijk onderwijs

lida sies *voorlichter*
[PRIVÉ 010 421 09 30] [FAX PRIVÉ 010 421 09 30]

STADSKANTOOR POSTBUS 70014
RODEZAND 18 3000 KS ROTTERDAM
tel [010] 417 32 05 fax [010] 414 31 62

1. **DOMINICCI** （Brazil） Lighting consultant 照明コンサルタント CD, D: Silvio Silva Junior CD: Mirian Hatori
2. **EVERGREEN** （Germany） Horticulture 園芸 CD, D: Detlef Behr DF: Büro für Kommunikationsdesign
3. **GALICHIA MEDICAL GROUP** （USA） Heart surgery 心臓外科医 CD, AD, D: Sonia Greteman D: James Strange DF: Greteman Group
4. **IPR** （Netherlands） Internet provider インターネット CD, AD, D, I, DF: Limage Dangereuse
5. **DSO** （Netherlands） Education service 教育サービス CD, AD, D, DF: Limage Dangereuse

1 2
3
4 5

b³
blumenthal

bürobedarf
büromaschinen
büromöbel

bernd blumenthal

b3 blumenthal
paul-langen-straße 44
5300 bonn 3

fon 02 28-43 05 50
fax 02 28-43 13 74

yanehiro inc.

133 Ridgeway *Road*
Hillsborough
California 94010

O:415.343.6910   H:415.347.5875   F:415.343.5853

lıl‖ıı En Route ı‖ıı

*Full Service Mailing
Distribution and Warehousing*

lıl‖ıı En Route ı‖ıı

700 Touhy Avenue, Elk Grove, Illinois 60007–4930
Telephone 708.439.8621 Facsimile 708.439.8617

Robert C. Losey
Vice President

Luciano Seregni
Amministratore Unico

P.A.T. s.r.l.
Promos Advanced Technologies
00187 Roma, Via Barberini 50
Tel. (06) 4825151 r.a. Telefax (06) 4827456
Telex 620055

PROMOS ADVANCED TECHNOLOGIES

Wieler Objektbau GmbH

Immobilienanlagen

Erhard David
Verkaufsleiter

Büro (0 71 81) 8 01-1 60
Mobil (01 72) 7 39 02 54
Fax (0 71 81) 8 01-1 68

Privat (0 71 81) 8 01-1 05

Immobilienanlagen
Wohn-, Gewerbe- und
Industriebau
Schlüsselfertige Objekte
Grundstücks- und
Projektentwicklung
Planen-Bauen-Vertrieb

Robert-Mayer-Straße 10
73660 Urbach

1. **b³ BLUMENTHAL** (Germany) Office supplies 事務用品 CD, D: Detlef Behr DF: Büro für Kommunikationsdesign
2. **JAN YANEHIRO** (USA) Media personality タレント CD: Richard Shiro AD, D: Traci Shiro DF: A Small Ad Shop
3. **EN ROUTE** (USA) Direct mail distribution ダイレクト メール CD: Mark Oldach D: Jennifer Wyville DF: Mark Oldach Design, Ltd.
4. **PAT. PROMOS ADVANCED TECHNOLOGIES** (USA) Advanced technology 先端技術 AD, D: Andrea Greco DF: Andrea Greco Design Studio
5. **WIELER OBJEKTBAU GMBH** (Germany) Real estate 不動産 CD, AD, D, I, CW: Udo Würth DF: Faktor, Design & Funktion

1 2
3
4 5

1. **MARZENA** （USA） Photographer's representation 写真 CD, AD, D: Robert Bergman-Ungar DF: Bergman-Ungar Associates

2. **KINETIC ART AND BUSINESS, INC.** （USA） Artists representation アーティスト CD, AD, D: Robert Bergman-Ungar DF: Bergman-Ungar Associates

3. **JONAH COMMUNICATIONS, INC.** （USA） Advertising sales representation 広告 CD, AD, D: Robert Bergman-Ungar DF: Bergman-Ungar Associates

1
2
3

1. **THE FORREST COMPANY** （USA） Environmental land analysis 土地開発研究 CD, AD, D: James Picquelle DF: Aloha Printing

2. **PAULA MONTE** （USA） Psychic consultant サイキック コンサルタント D: Colleen McGunnigle DF: Nouveaux Visages

3. **DR. IGOR HASAJ, MARIBOR** （Slovenia） Dentist 歯科医 AD, D: Edi Berk DF: Krog, Ljubljana

4. **ALMA MIDDLETON** （USA） Massage therapist マッサージ師 CD, AD, D, I, CW: Alan Middleton DF: Middleton Performance Marketing

5. **TOWN & COUNTRY SEAFOOD** （USA） Catering ケータリング CD, AD, D, I, CW: Lani Isherwood DF: La Visage

6. **ALL SEASONS SALON** （USA） Hair salon ヘア サロン D, I: Colleen McGunnigle DF: Nouveaux Visages

1 2 3

4 5 6

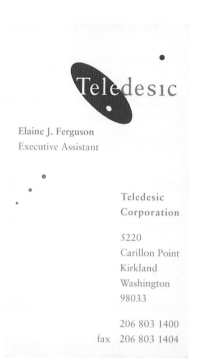

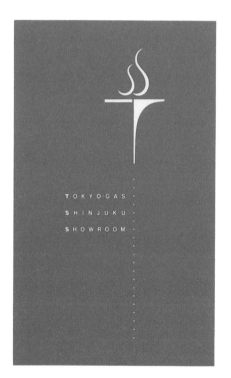

1. **METRO QUADRADO** （Brazil） Horticulture 園芸 CD, D: Silvio Silva Junior CD: Mirian Hatori DF: Studio Lumen Design

2. **TELEDISC CORPORATION** （USA） Satellite communications 衛星通信サービス
AD, D: Jack Anderson D: Leo Raymundo DF: Hornall Anderson Design Works, Inc.

3. **SANGYO YUSO** （Japan） Transportation services 輸送 AD, D: Junichi Naito DF: J・Family

4. **URBAN COMMUNICATIONS INC.** （Japan） Event planning イベント企画 D: Douglas Doolittle DF: Douglas Design Inc.

5. **EVAG. PAPAGEORGIU** （Greece） Dentist 歯科医 CD, AD, D: Leonidas Kanellos DF: Leonidas Kanellos Design Group

QuadraSeps

Glen Rhoades

1963 H Street
Fresno, CA 93721
209-485-CYMK
Fax 209-264-9876
Modem/BBS 209-237-6226

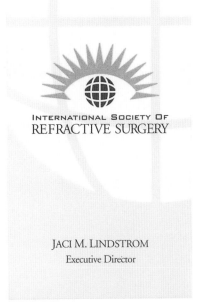

INTERNATIONAL SOCIETY OF
REFRACTIVE SURGERY

JACI M. LINDSTROM
Executive Director

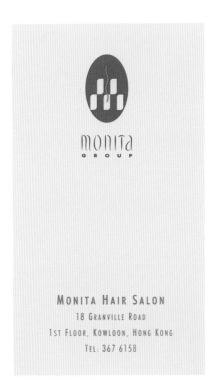

MONITA HAIR SALON
18 GRANVILLE ROAD
1ST FLOOR, KOWLOON, HONG KONG
TEL: 367 6158

Tormen
e figli

impresa
costruzioni

CH– 6675 Cevio
Telefono
privato 093 96 19 17

PHILLIPS EYE INSTITUTE

2215 PARK AVENUE

MINNEAPOLIS, MINNESOTA

U.S.A. 55404

TEL: 1-612-336-7575

FAX: 1-612-336-5530

CENTER
PLAZA

Lauria Brennan
Director of Retail Leasing

Beacon Management Company
Three Center Plaza
Boston, Massachusetts 02108
T: 617.227.6743 · F: 617.227.0523

1. **QUADRA SEPS** （USA） Computer services コンピューター サービス CD, AD: Charles Shields D: Juan Vega DF: Shields Design
2. **INTERNATIONAL SOCIETY OF REFRACTIVE SURGERY** （USA） Eye surgery 眼科医 CD, AD: Sonia Greteman D: Todd Gimlin DF: Greteman Group
3. **MONITA GROUP** （Hong Kong） Beauty school 美容学校 CD, AD: Kan Tai-keung AD, D: Eddy Yu Chi Kong
    D: Joyce Ho Ngai Sing DF: Kan Tai-keung Design & Associates Ltd.
4. **RENZO TORMEN** （Switzerland） Construction 建設 CD, AD, D: Oberholzer Tagli Knobel
5. **BEACON MANAGEMENT COMPANY** （USA） Real estate 不動産 CD: Kathryn Klein D: Tim McGrath / Maite Tome DF: After Midnight, Inc.

1 2 3

4 5

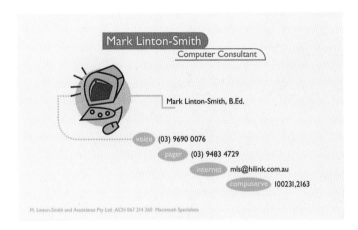

1. **MARK LINTON SMITH** （Australia） Computer consultant コンピューター コンサルタント
   AD: Andrew Hoyne D: Anna Svigos I: Angela Ho DF: Andrew Hoyne Design

2. **JUN MAEKAWA** （Japan） Writer ライター D: Hirofumi Akiyama DF: Basic, Inc.

3. **GRAEBEL FINE ART** （USA） Fine art storage, removals 美術品保管 CD: Pattie Belle Hastings AD, D: Bjorn Akselsen DF: Icehouse Design

4. **POMEGRANATE CENTER** （USA） Non-profit organization 慈善団体 CD, AD, D: Rick Eiber DF: Rick Eiber Design

5. **KANSAS HEALTH FOUNDATION** （USA） Non-profit organization 慈善団体 CD, AD, D: Sonia Greteman D: James Strange DF: Greteman Group

1 2
3
4 5

代表取締役
中島春喜

株式会社インハウス
〒106 東京都港区西麻布2-15-7 東一ビル3F
Tel:03-3498-9811 Fax:03-3498-9801

GREEN CITY

Alexander Gröger

718 599 4867

65 South 8th St. #4
Brooklyn, NY 11211

DANIEL L. BARNETT
CHIEF OPERATING OFFICER

DIRECT: 206 224 1637
MAIN: 206 654 5300
FAX: 206 382 6615
INTERNET:
danb@xactdata.com

XACTDATA CORPORATION
ONE UNION SQUARE
600 UNIVERSITY STREET
SUITE 911
SEATTLE WA 98101

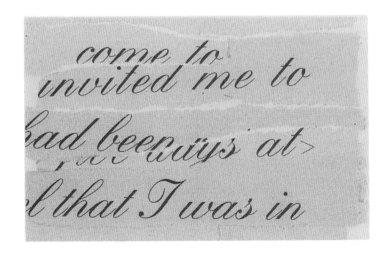

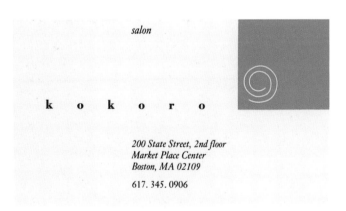

salon

k o k o r o

200 State Street, 2nd floor
Market Place Center
Boston, MA 02109

617. 345. 0906

1. **IN HOUSE** （Japan） Interior consultant　**インテリア プロデューサー**　AD: Masaaki Hiromura　D: Takafumi Kusagaya　DF: Hiromura Design Office

2. **GREEN CITY** （USA） Horticulture　**園芸**　CD, AD: Stefan Sagmeister　D, I: Veronica Oh　DF: Sagmeister Inc.

3. **XACTDATA CORPORATION** （USA） Distribution system back-up　**バック アップ システム**
AD, D: Jack Anderson　D: Jana Wilson / Lisa Cerveny / Julie Keenan　DF: Hornall Anderson Design Works, Inc.

4. **PETER U. HOUT** （Netherlands） Artist　**アーティスト**　D: Van Hout

5. **SALON KOKORO** （USA） Hair salon　**ヘア サロン**　CD, AD, D: Jane Cuthbertson　D: Ted Groves　DF: Myriad Design

1 2
3
4 5

Greenhouse

GREENHOUSE

PRODUCTIONS

P.O. BOX 6283

KAMUELA, HAWAII

96743   Christine Eason

(808) 885-4272
tel

(808) 885-4594
fax

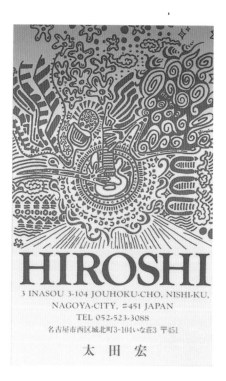

1. **PLANET HAIR** （USA） Hair salon ヘア サロン CD, AD, D: Sonia Greteman DF: Greteman Group

2. **GREENHOUSE PRODUCTION** （USA） Financial management 財務マネージメント CD, AD, D: Stan Evenson DF: Evenson Design Group

3. **HEART OF LOS ANGELES YOUTH** （USA） Children's welfare organization 児童保護団体 CD, AD: Stan Evenson D: Angie Boothroyd DF: Evenson Design Group

4. **PET NET** （USA） Pet care services ペット ケア CD, AD: Stan Evenson D: Tricia Rauen DF: Evenson Design Group

5. **HIROSHI OTA** （Japan） Vocalist ボーカリスト CD, AD, D, I: Tomio Shinohara DF: Voice Corporation

1. **ESCOLA DE SAMBA** （USA） Dance instruction ダンス講師 CD, AD, D: Ellie Leacock DF: Art Stuff

2. **HUNGRY CAMPER** （USA） Catering ケータリング CD, AD, D, I: John Sayles DF: Sayles Graphic Design

3. **JILL DUPLEIX** （Australia） Writer ライター AD: Andrew Hoyne D, I, DF; Andrew Hoyne Design

1 2

3

1. **DR. JACOB HORWITZ D. M. D** （Israel） Dentist 歯科医 D, I: Dina Shoham

2. **TSUKAMOTO EYE CLINIC** （Japan） Eye surgery 眼科医 AD, D: Sumihiro Takeuchi DF: Sumihiro Takeuchi Design Office

3. **TSUJI DENTAL CLINIC** （Japan） Dentist 歯科医 AD, D: Sumihiro Takeuchi DF: Sumihiro Takeuchi Design Office

1

2 3

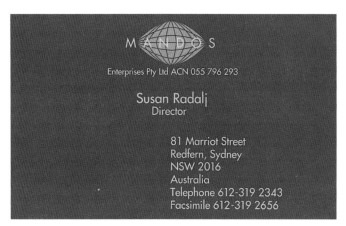

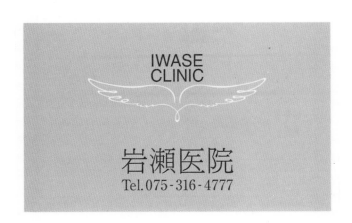

1. **MANDOS** (Australia) Distribution 流通 AD: Andrew Hoyne D, DF: Andrew Hoyne Design
2. **ROCKET BOY BLUE** (Australia) Event planning イベント企画 AD, D: Andrew Hoyne D: Anna Svigos DF: Andrew Hoyne Design
3. **IWASE CLINIC** (Japan) Psychiatry 精神科医 AD, D: Sumihiro Takeuchi DF: Sumihiro Takeuchi Design Office
4. **PAUL BARGEHR** (Austria) Massage therapist マッサージ師 AD, D: Sigi Ramoser I: Peter Felder

1
2
3 4

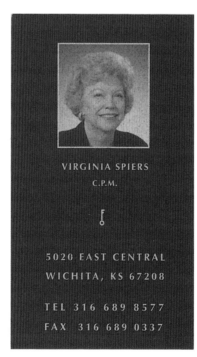

1. **PRECIOUS MEMORIES** （USA） Funeral music service 葬儀用ミュージック サービス D: Glenn Sweitzer DF: Fresh Design

2. **ANITA FREY** （USA） Real estate 不動産 CD, AD: Sonia Greteman D: James Strange DF: Greteman Group

3. **WISCONSIN ACADEMY** （USA） Academic training アカデミック トレーニング CD, D: Jane Jenkins / Tom Jenkins DF: The Design Foundry

4. **MELROSE CONSULTING** （USA） Consulting コンサルティング CD: Melodye Demastus AD: Eric Rickabaugh D: Tina Zientarski DF: Rickabaugh Graphics

5. **THE GEORGIAN HOTEL** （USA） Hotel ホテル CD, AD: Petrula Vrontikis D: Christina Hsiao DF: Vrontikis Design Office

1 2 3

4 5

Lee Marks

11 East 73rd Street
New York, NY 10021
212-472-2565
Fax: 212-288-9439

American Organization
of Nurse Executives

One North Franklin Street
34th Floor
Chicago, IL 60606
TEL 312.422.2811
FAX 312.422.4503

Joan Riebock
Director, Education
and Meetings

mail
Cees en Karin van Bockel
Hertelaan 70
NL.5704 DS Helmond

courses/training
Cees van Bockel [IADS 10750]
t 31 [0]492 - 51 76 80

general affairs
Lisette Sprengers en Goof Rutten
t 31 [0]40 - 283 95 37
f 31 [0]40 - 283 91 36
Plaza@euronet.nl

planning/events
John Serton
t 31 [0]73- 622 11 73

scuba Jones is member of the IADS,
international association of diving schools - NL

ochi miyuki
writer/planner

越智みゆき

SATOKO ISEKI STYLIST

井関智子

401, 1-8-5 Hiroo, Shibuya-ku,
Tokyo 150, Japan
Telephone & Fax (03) 3498-1496
〒150 東京都渋谷区広尾1-8-5-401

STUDIO BELLS

依田保雄
作曲・編曲・選曲

スタジオ・ベルズ
東京都中野区中央2-44-9
レオパレス中野坂上108 〒164
PHONE 03-3369-0917

〒565 吹田市千里山東1-18-8 #201
phone & facsimile 06.339.0642

---

1. **CAMERAWORKS** （USA） Photo archive 写真保管 CD, AD, D: Yoshifumi Fujii
2. **AMERICAN ORGANIZATION OF NURSE EXECUTIVES** （USA） Non-profit organization 慈善団体
   CD: Mark Oldach D: Jennifer Wyville DF: Mark Oldach Design, Ltd.
3. **SCUBA JONES** （Netherlands） Scuba diving school スキューバ ダイビング スクール D: Goof Rutten DF: Plaza Ontwerpers
4. **SATOKO ISEKI** （Japan） Stylist スタイリスト D: Kazumasa Watanabe
5. **STUDIO BELLS** （Japan） Composer 作曲家 AD, D: Fukushi Okubo DF: Fukushi Okubo Design Office
6. **MIYUKI OCHI** （Japan） Writer ライター CD, AD, D: Sachi Sawada DF: Moss Design Unit

1 2 3
4 5 6

1. **CHRISTINA LUNA** （USA） Child care チャイルド ケア CD, AD, D: Al Luna DF: Luna Design

2. **CHEVEUX COURTS** （Japan） Hair and make-up salon ヘアメーク サロン CD, AD, D: Satoshi Matsuda DF: Face Inc.

3. **TINEKE HEY CONSULTANTS** （Netherlands） Head hunter ヘッド ハンター CD, D: Ron Van Der Vlugt DF: Designers Company

4. **THE FINISHING TOUCH** （USA） Finishing service フィニッシング サービス CD, AD, D, I: John Sayles DF: Sayles Graphic Design

5. **GIESING TEAM** （Germany） Sound studio 音楽スタジオ CD: Thomas Feicht AD: Christine Pfaff D: Nina Schaarschmidt DF: Trust

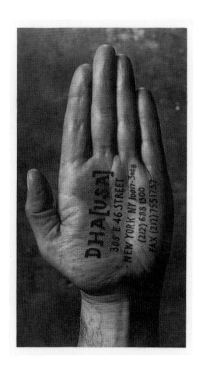

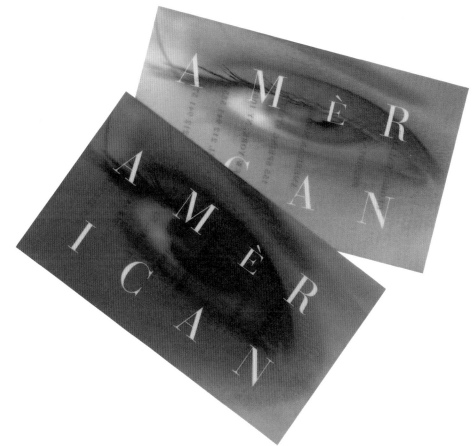

1. **ALMA MECATTAF** （France） Scriptwriter 台本作家 CD, AD, D: Paul Hage-Chahine

2. **NICHOLAS MORLEY** （Australia） Hair and make-up artist ヘアメーク アーティスト AD: Andrew Hoyne P: Rob Blackburn D, DF: Andrew Hoyne Design

3. **DHA [USA]** （USA） Consulting コンサルティング CD, AD: Stefan Sagmeister P: Tom Schierlitz DF: Sagmeister Inc.

4. **AMERICAN MODEL** （USA） Modeling agency モデル事務所 CD, AD, D: Robert Bergman-Ungar DF: Bergman-Ungar Associates

1 2 3
4

Barry Varshay
LOAN OFFICER

420 Bullard, Suite 101 • Clovis, California 93612
800-266-2550 • 209-323-2550 • Fax: 209-323-2543

Don Peterson, CPA
Associate
310.556.6609

 GELFAND, RENNERT & FELDMAN

A Division	Certified	1880 Century	Telephone:
of Coopers	Public	Park East	310.553.1707
& Lybrand	Accountants	Suite 900	Telecopier:
		Los Angeles,	310.557.8412
		California	
		90067	

INSURESMART
The Intelligent Way To Insure

4420 Hotel Circle Ct., Suite 150  *San Diego, California 92108*

Telephone 619.260.1111 *Facsimile 619.293.3580*

DAVID PETER DUENAS
President

梁
振
英
測
量
師
行

梁
振
英

香港測量師學會資深會員
英國皇家特許資深測量師
董事總經理

香港中環
怡和大廈10樓
電話：507 0507
電傳：530 1555
直線：507 0500

Center
for the
Study
of
Social
Policy

Tom Joe
Director

1250 Eye Street, NW
Suite 503
Washington, DC
20005-3922
Fax **202 371-1472**
Voice **202 371-1565**

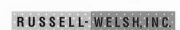

Evelyn A. Evans
MANAGER ADMINISTRATION

1660 SOUTH
AMPHLETT BLVD.
SUITE 219
SAN MATEO
CA 94402
TELEPHONE
415 312 0700
FACSIMILE
415 312 9007

1. **HERITAGE PLAZA MORTGAGE, INC.** (USA) Mortgage lending ローン会社 CD, AD, D: Charles Shields DF: Shields Design
2. **GELFAND, RENNERT, FELDMAN & BROWN** (USA) Public accountant 公認会計士 CD, AD: Stan Evenson D: Tricia Rauen DF: Evenson Design Group
3. **INSURESMART** (USA) Insurance broker 保険 CD, AD, D: Scott Mires DF: Mires Design, Inc.
4. **C. Y. LEUNG & COMPANY LIMITED** (Hong Kong) Real estate 不動産 CD, AD: Kan Tai-keung AD, D: Freeman Lau Siu Hong / Eddy Yu Chi Kong
    D: Veronica Cheung Lai Sheung DF: Kan Tai-keung Design & Associates Ltd.
5. **CENTER FOR THE STUDY OF SOCIAL POLICY** (USA) Social policy think tank 社会政策
    AD, D: Samuel G. Shelton / Jeffrey S. Fabian DF: Kinetik Communication Graphics, Inc.
6. **RUSSELL-WELSH, INCORPORATED** (USA) Public relations 宣伝 CD, AD: Lawrence Bender D: Timothy Lau DF: Lawrence Bender & Associates

1 2
3 4
5 6

JOHN J. SKIBA
President and
Chief Executive Officer

Sun Country Airlines

2520 Pilot Knob Rd. Suite No. 250
Mendota Heights, Minnesota 55120
Tel 612.681.3900 Fax 612.681.3970

hammered dulcimer ◎ performance & instruction

tina bergmann p.o. box 241
richfield, ohio 44286-0241
tel / fax: 216.659.4081

American
Asset
Management,
Inc.

Registered Investment Advisor

Interchange North • 300 South Highway 169
Suite 250 • St. Louis Park, MN 55426-9778

Stephen C. North
Financial Consultant
Tel. (612) 540-0195

(800) 221-8176 • Fax (612) 540-0282
Securities sold through AAM Securities, Inc.
Service since 1981

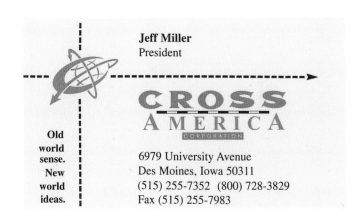

Jeff Miller
President

CROSS AMERICA
CORPORATION

Old
world
sense.
New
world
ideas.

6979 University Avenue
Des Moines, Iowa 50311
(515) 255-7352 (800) 728-3829
Fax (515) 255-7983

Dr. Erich Schwarzmann
Praxis für Gross- und Kleintiere

A-6861 Alberschwende · Rohnen 785
T 05579 4738 · F 05579 4493-6
Österreich +43 5579 4738

Erich Schwarzmann
prakt. Tierarzt

PRODUCTIONS BY
CLASSIC EVENTS

SANDRA L. SICKLER
EVENT PRODUCTION CONSULTANT
(714) 362-8413
23974 Aliso Creek Road Suite 365 Laguna Niguel Ca. 92677

1. **SUN COUNTRY AIRLINES** (USA) Charter airline 航空会社 CD, AD: John Reger D: Todd Spichke DF: Design Center

2. **TINA BERGMANN** (USA) Musician ミュージシャン CD, D, I: Patty J. Palazzo AD: Molly J. Zakrajsek DF: Triple Seven Design

3. **AMERICAN ASSET MANAGEMENT, INC.** (USA) Financial advisor 財務アドバイザー CD, AD: John Reger D: Sherwin Schwartzrock DF: Design Center

4. **CROSS AMERICA** (USA) Financial services 財務サービス CD, AD, D, I: John Sayles DF: Sayles Graphic Design

5. **DR. ERICH SCHWARZMANN** (Austria) Veterinarian 獣医 CD, AD: Harry Metzler D: Sabine Linder DF: Harry Metzler Artdesign

6. **CLASSIC EVENTS** (USA) Promotional production プロモーショナル プロダクション CD, AD, D: James Picquelle DF: Aloha Printing

1 2
3 4
5 6

Denis Courtemanche

Valiquette
& Associés

Avocats

625, boul. René-Lévesque ouest
Bureau 800
Montréal (QC) H3B 1R2

Téléphone: (514) 874-0491
Télécopieur: (514) 874-0489

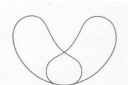

理事長 小池 欣一

財団法人 骨髄移植推進財団
〒160 東京都新宿区新宿1-4-8
電話03-3355-5041 ファクシミリ03-3355-5090

GÜNTHER LOACKER KEG

BRUNNENAU 7 6890 LUSTENAU

TELEFON & FAX : 05577 / 87780

LEICHTER LERNEN

Bill Thompson
169 Norfolk Avenue Number Nine
Boston Massachusetts 02119
617 445 8009

Stylist
間野利江子

un peu
bis

アンプービス・151 東京都渋谷区代々木5-6-12 小澤ビルB1 Tel (03) 3465-3479
アンプー・150 東京都渋谷区神宮前3-7-1 マリオンビル2F Tel (03) 3497-0973

1. **VALIQUETTE & ASSOCIÉS** (Canada) Law practice 弁護士 AD, D: Rolf Harder DF: Rolf Harder & Assoc. Inc.
2. **THE JAPAN MARROW DONOR FOUNDATION** (Japan) Medical service 医療 AD, D: Noriko Hara D: Rentaro Harada
3. **GÜNTER LOACKER KEG** (Austria) Educational materials 教育用品 CD, AD, D: Sigi Ramoser
4. **BILL THOMPSON** (USA) Artist アーティスト CD, AD, D: Jane Cuthbertson DF: Forsythe Design
5. **UN PEU** (Japan) Hair salon ヘア サロン D: Akihiko Tsukamoto

1 2
3
4 5

1. **PRODEO** (Finland) Consulting コンサルティング D: Viktor Kaltala DF: Viktorno Design Oy

2. **YUMIKO YAZAKI** (Japan) Pianist ピアニスト AD, D: Junichi Naito DF: J・Family

3. **TOKYO BEAUTY CENTER** (Japan) Beauty salon エステティック サロン AD, D: Jun Takechi

4. **THE ERAS CENTER** (USA) Children's welfare organization 児童保護団体 CD, AD: Stan Evenson D: Ken Loh DF: Evenson Design Group

5. **NIKKI GOLDSTEIN** (Australia) Stylist スタイリスト AD, D: Andrew Hoyne D: Amanda McPherson P: Rob Blackburn DF: Andrew Hoyne Design

good

You feel

feel

Make

You feel

Make

hair Jürgen Witzgall [Inhaber]

Hans Berkmann

Eigen Art

Quellenstraße 5   6900 Bregenz   T 05574/52909

Cosmetics

Cosmetics

Robert F. Hernandez
Investigator
Post Office Box 9910
San Diego, CA 92109
Phone 619 488-4044

RONNIE S. STANGLER, M.D.
Psychiatry 1425 Western Avenue, Suite 101
Seattle, Washington 98101-2036
Tel 206.622.3069 Fax 206.622.8150

OPPOSITE PAGE: **EIGEN ART** （Austria）Hair and make-up studio　ヘアメーク スタジオ
CD, AD, D, I: Sigi Ramoser CD: Sandro Scherling D, I: Stefan Gassner CW: Hermann Brändle DF: Atelier für Text und Gestaltung

1. **LUNARDI STUDIO FÜR BRAUTMODE** （Austria）Wedding fashion studio　ウェディング ファッション
CD, AD, D: Sigi Ramoser AD, D: Stefan Gassner D: Sandro Scherling DF: Atelier für Text und Gestaltung

2. **MIDLAND RESEARCH** （USA）Investigation and research　探偵　CD, AD, D: José Serrano I: Tracy Sabin DF: Mires Design, Inc.

3. **RONNIE STANGLER** （USA）Psychiatry　精神科医　D: Doug Keyes DF: A / D

1

2 3

藤 原 　真理子
Mariko Fujiwara

〒542　大阪市中央区南船場3-11-27
日宝シルバービル5F
Phone. 06-243-3243
Fax. 　06-243-3342

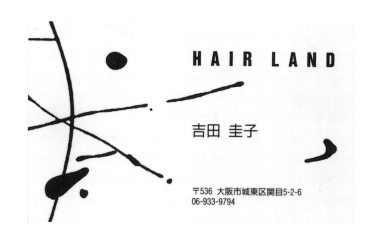

吉田 　圭子

〒536　大阪市城東区関目5-2-6
06-933-9794

PACIFIC PRIVILEGE

Ken Barrett
CONSULTANT

2608, Shell Tower, Times Square, 1 Matheson St, Causeway Bay, Hong Kong
Telephone: 506 3901　Facsimile: 506 2900

代表
劉 美也子

エムズセレクション（株式会社B・B・C）
100 東京都千代田区永田町2-17-11-503
Tel (03) 3593-3108　Fax (03) 3595-3699

Dean E. Cama

Original Musical
Compositions and
Arrangements for
Film and Theatre

1. **MITY** （Japan）Event planner イベント企画　CD, AD, D: Junko Kitamura　DF: Tomboy Pro

2. **HAIR LAND** （Japan）Hair salon ヘア サロン　AD, D: Ciro Moritan

3. **MEMBERSHIP ETC LIMITED** （Hong Kong）Leisure club レジャー クラブ　CD: Kan Tai-keung
AD, D, I: Eddy Yu Chi Kong　AD, D: Freeman Lau Siu Hong　DF: Kan Tai-keung Design & Associates Ltd.

4. **M'S SELECTION** （Japan）Planner プランナー　D: Akihiko Tsukamoto

5. **DEAN E. CAMA** （USA）Composer 作曲家　D: Colleen McGunnigle　DF: Nouveaux Visages

1 2
3
4 5

fos ihos

rehearsal studios

8, LAMIAS str. Athens
tel: 64.65.895, 64.27.240
fax: 64.27.240
mobile: 094 305.845

Croatia · Czech Rep · Germany · Hungary · Macedonia · Poland · Romania · Russia

Austria · Belarus · Bosnia · Bulgaria · Canada

Slovakia · Slovenia · Ukraine · United States

CARGOLINE

Hannes Glatzer
Zollabteilung

Freudenauer Hafenstraße 20 - 22
A-1020 Wien
Tel (43-1) 727 000
Fax (43-1) 727 00 33

BRITE.

TEL 316 631 3053
FAX 316 631 3400
NET barbara.rice@brite.com

9229 E. 37th Street North
Wichita, KS 67226-2011
OFFICES WORLDWIDE

BARBARA RICE
Account Manager
Communication Services

Clean-Up Technology

Stacey Schecter
Office Manager

3228 Nebraska Ave   *California State*
Santa Monica   *Contractor*
CA 90404   *License # 589424*
Tel 213/828-4844   *Hazardous Substance*
Fax 213/828-1298   *Certificate*

OPTIKA MIRJE
BARON&BARON d.o.o.
Trg MDB 2, 61000 LJUBLJANA, Slovenija
tel.: 061/125 60 59, fax.: 061/125 60 83

Baron & BARON

SEAFIELD

Seafield Holdings
Limited

Regis House
Gordon Road
Canterbury
Kent, CT1 3PJ

Tel: 0227 787777

Fax: 0227 787708

Lyle J Noble
Managing Director

1. **FOS & IHOS**　(Greece)　Rehearsal studio　リハーサル スタジオ　CD, AD, D: Leonidas Kanellos　DF: Leonidas Kanellos Design Group
2. **CARGOLINE**　(Austria)　Transportation service　輸送　CD: Lothar Ämilian Heinzle　DF: ACC-Heinzle Vie
3. **BRITE**　(USA)　Communication service　コミュニケーション サービス　CD, AD: Sonia Greteman　D: James Strange　DF: Greteman Group
4. **CLEAN-UP TECHNOLOGY**　(USA)　Environmental contractor　土建　CD, AD: Stan Evenson　D: Tricia Rauen　DF: Evenson Design Group
5. **BARON & BARON**　(Slovenia)　Optical services　オプティカル サービス　CD, AD, D: Sašo Urukalo　DF: Stvarnik d. j. j.
6. **SEAFIELD**　(UK)　Transportation service　輸送　CD, AD, D: John Nash　DF: John Nash & Friends

1 2
3 4
5 6

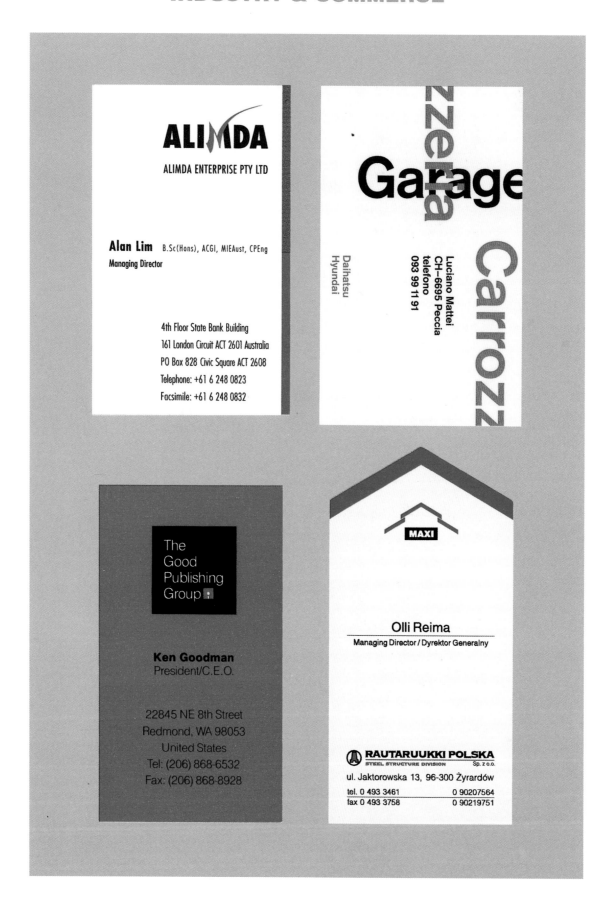

OPPOSITE PAGE: **TOTO NCG** (USA) Bathrooms supplier バスルーム システム CD, AD, D: Stefan Sagmeister D: Veronica Oh P: Michael Grimm DF: Sagmeister Inc.

1. **ALIMDA ENTERPRISE PTY LTD.** (Australia) Trading company 貿易 AD, D: Linda Fu DF: Linda Fu Design

2. **LUCIANO MATTEI PECCIA** (Switzerland) Auto repairs 自動車修理 CD, AD, D: Oberholzer Tagli Knobel

3. **THE GOOD PUBLISHING GROUP** (USA) Software development ソフトウェア CD, AD, D: Greg Walters DF: Greg Walters Design

4. **RAUTARUUKKI POLSKA** (Poland) Roof systems ルーフ システム CD, AD, D: Tadeusz Piechura CW: Mariusz Wieczorek DF: Atelier Tadeusz Piechura

1 2
3 4

TOTO

TOTO

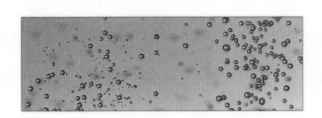

TOTO

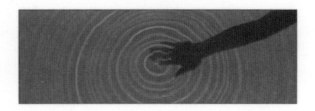

TOTO

TOTO

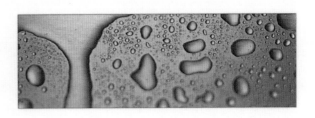

TOTO

toto kiki usa, inc.

ken wijaya
engineering manager

415 west taft avenue unit a
orange, california 92665
telephone +1 714 282 8686
facsimile +1 714 282 1541

TOTO

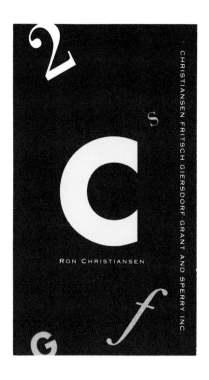

1. **SEASONS** （USA） Apparel maker アパレル メーカー CD, D: Molly J. Zakrajsek AD: Patty J. Palazzo DF: Triple Seven Design

2. **BESS CORPORATION** （Japan） Bio-ecology system supplier バイオエコロジー システム AD: Kenji Koga DF: Collective Yellow Artist Inc.

3. **CHRISTIANSEN FRITSCH GIERSDORF GRANT & SPERRY, INC.** （USA） Direct marketing ダイレクトマーケティング
AD, D: Jack Anderson D: David Bates DF: Hornall Anderson Design Works, Inc.

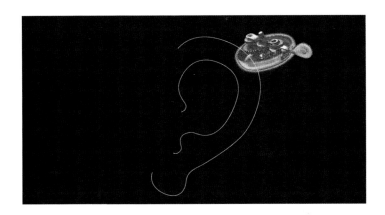

marketing & communicatie

(v l i (e) g e r)

Anneke Vlieger

heemraadssingel 245
3023 CD **rotterdam**
tel 010 476 16 92
fax 010 476 73 69
mobile 06 52 75 72 36

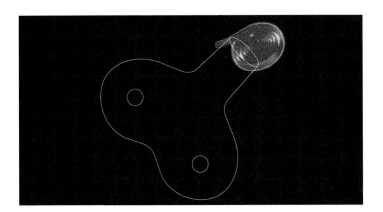

marketing & communicatie

(v l i (e) g e r)

Anneke Vlieger

heemraadssingel 245
3023 CD **rotterdam**
tel 010 476 16 92
fax 010 476 73 69
mobile 06 52 75 72 36

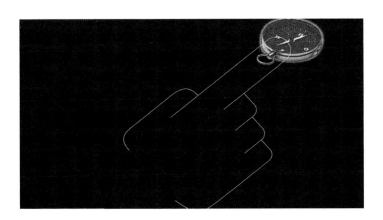

marketing & communicatie

(v l i (e) g e r)

Anneke Vlieger

heemraadssingel 245
3023 CD **rotterdam**
tel 010 476 16 92
fax 010 476 73 69
mobile 06 52 75 72 36

1. **VLIEGER** (Netherlands) Marketing マーケティング CD, AD, D, I: Limage Dangereuse P: Hans De Jong

1
2
3

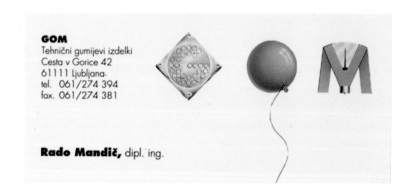

1. **BARTLETT WINERY** (USA) Winery ワイン工場 CD, AD, D: Louise Fili DF: Louise Fili Ltd.

2. **HOUSE OF LORDS** (USA) Trading company 貿易 CD, AD, D: Ellie Leacock P: Andy Stracuzzi DF: Art Stuff

3. **FACELLI WINERY** (USA) Winery ワイン工場 D: Giorgio Davanzo P: Bob Michels DF: Giorgio Davanzo Design

4. **FIORUCCI** (Italy) Apparel maker アパレル メーカー CD: Elio Fiorucci AD, DF: Fiorucci Design Studio

5. **GOM** (Slovenia) Rubber goods manufacturer ゴム製品メーカー AD, D: Edi Berk I: Zlato Drčar DF: Krog, Ljubljana

```
1
2  3
4  5
```

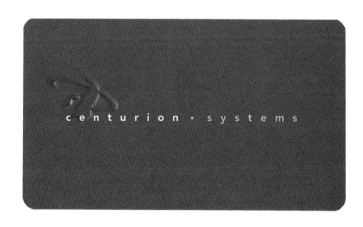

1. **PAVLOVA INTERNATIONAL COMPANY LIMITED** （Hong Kong） Cosmetics 化粧品
CD, AD: Kan Tai-keung AD, D: Clement Yick Tat Wa DF: Kan Tai-keung Design & Associates Ltd.

2. **METROPOLIS FINE CONFECTIONS** （USA） Confectionery maker 洋菓子 CD, AD, D: Marcia Romanuck DF: The Design Company

3. **CENTURIAN SYSTEMS** （USA） Programming プログラミング CD, AD, D: Mike Melia DF: Melia Design Group

1
2
3

1. **XINET, INC.** （USA）Software **ソフトウェア** CD, AD, D: Earl Gee I: Robert Pastrana DF: Gee+Chung Design

2. **WINNING VISIONS** （USA）Marketing **マーケティング** CD, AD, D: Sonia Greteman D: Jo Quillin DF: Greteman Group

1. **DELEO CLAY TILE CO.** （USA） Roof tile manufacturer 屋根材メーカー CD, AD, D: José Serrano I: Nancy Stahl DF: Mires Design, Inc.

2. **GREAT PACIFIC TRADING COMPANY** （USA） Trading company 貿易 CD, AD, D: Charles Shields I: Doug Hansen DF: Shields Design

3. **WATSON FURNITURE COMPANY** （USA） Office furniture manufacturer オフィス家具メーカー
AD, D: Jack Anderson D: Mary Hermes / Leo Raymundo DF: Hornall Anderson Design Works, Inc.

4. **J2 COLLECTION** （USA） Gift wrap manufacturer 包装紙メーカー CD, D: Jane Jenkins / Tom Jenkins DF: The Design Foundry

5. **STEPHEN KOWALSKI** （USA） Clock manufacture 時計メーカー CD: Stephen Kowalski AD, D: Janèl Apple D: Krysten Bonzelet
P: David Hayashida / George Post CW: Pamela Shandrik DF: Kowalski Designworks, Inc.

6. **LOVEABLE CHOCOLATES** （USA） Confectionery maker 洋菓子 CD, AD: Rick Eiber D: David Balzer DF: Rick Eiber Design

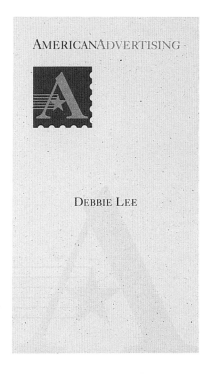

CHRIS
STEVENS

Manufacturer's
Representative

14150
NE 20th Street
Suite 366
Bellevue, WA
98007
Fax 206 885 7106
206 885 7190

JOE CRAWFORD
GENERAL MANANGER
FEATHER & DOWN PROCESSING

LOCAL: (206)653-3696
SEATTLE: (206)743-1677
FAX: (206)659-4222

14524 40TH AVE. NE
MARYSVILLE, WA 98270-8903 USA

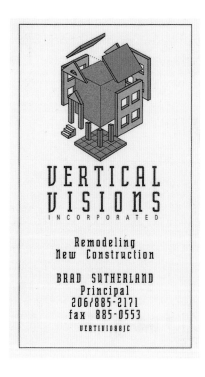

KATIE SIMS
Director, Communications

One Stimson Lane
Woodinville, WA 98072
206-488-4682
Fax 206-488-4657

1. **CHRIS STEVENS** (USA) Manufacturer's representation 製造業者 AD, D: Jack Anderson DF: Hornall Anderson Design Works, Inc.

2. **AMERICAN ADVERTISING** (USA) Marketing マーケティング CD, AD: Sonia Greteman D: James Strange DF: Greteman Group

3. **PACIFIC COAST FEATHER COMPANY** (USA) Feather goods manufacturer 羽毛用品メーカー
AD, D: Jack Anderson D: Julie Lock / Heidi Favour / Leo Raymundo I: Carolyn Vibbert DF: Hornall Anderson Design Works, Inc.

4. **VERTICAL VISIONS** (USA) Construction 建設 D, I: Robert M. Brünz DF: RM Brünz Studio

5. **COLUMBIA CREST WINERY** (USA) Winery ワイン工場 AD, D: John Hornall
D: Viola Lehr / Debra Hampton / Mary Chin Hutchison I: Jerry Nelson DF: Hornall Anderson Design Works, Inc.

1 2 3

4 5

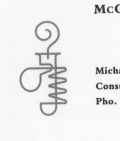

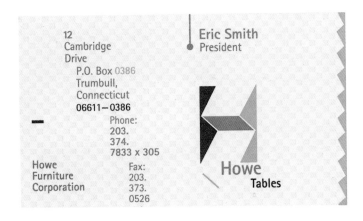

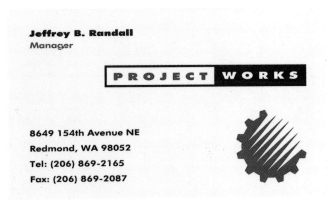

1. **ST. CROIX SENSORY, INC.** (USA) Engineering 工学 CD, AD: John Reger D: Sherwin Schwartzrock DF: Design Center

2. **HOMEWORKS** (USA) Construction management 建設 CD, AD, D, I: John Sayles DF: Sayles Graphic Design

3. **LOONBEDRIJF VAN DER LAAN** (Netherlands) Construction 建設 D: Ebel Kuipers

4. **McGINLEY ASSOCIATES** (USA) Engineering 工学 CD, AD: John Reger D: Sherwin Schwartzrock DF: Design Center

5. **HOWE TABLES - HOWE FURNITURE CORPORATION** (USA) Furniture manufacturer 家具メーカー D: Nancy Skolos DF: Skolos / Wedell, Inc.

6. **PROJECT WORKS** (USA) Software ソフトウェア CD, AD, D: Greg Walters DF: Greg Walters Design

1. **K2 SNOWBOARDS** （USA） Snowboard manufacturer スノーボード メーカー CD: Luke Edgar AD, D, I: Vittorio Costarella DF: Modern Dog

2. **I. A. BEDFORD** （USA） Textile manufacturer テキスタイル メーカー CD, AD, D, I: John Sayles DF: Sayles Graphic Design

3. **K2 SNOWBOARDS** （USA） Snowboard manufacturer スノーボード メーカー CD: Luke Edgar / Hayley Martin AD, D, I: George Estrada DF: Modern Dog

4. **3 BAGS FULL** （Australia） Bag manufacturer ランドリーバッグ メーカー AD, D: Andrew Hoyne I, DF: Andrew Hoyne Design

純米酢・味噌【醸造元】

ミヅホ株式会社

〒634 奈良県橿原市中町267番地

［電話］07442／2／3317

［ファクシミリ］07442／5／5844

代表取締役

大西 亮一

Ryoichi Ohnishi

登録商標

MIZUHO

Manufacture of Japanese Vinegar & Miso

創業明治10年

CYBER
TECHNOLOGIES INTERNATIONAL

Edward Harter
Software & Systems Development Director

Cyber Technologies International Co., Ltd.
304 Otake No.5 Bldg. 4-6 Daikyocho Shinjuku-ku Tokyo Japan 160
TEL : 03-3226-0961   FAX : 03-3226-0962   eharter@cyber.ad.jp

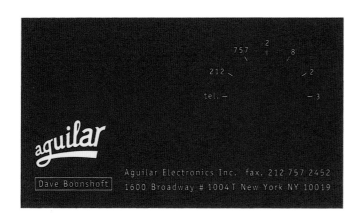

1. **MIZUHO CO., LTD.** (Japan) Food manufacturer 酢メーカー AD, D: Sumihiro Takeuchi DF: Sumihiro Takeuchi Design Office

2. **CYBER TECHNOLOGIES INTERNATIONAL CO., LTD.** (Japan) Internet provider インターネット AD, D: Minoru Murata DF: Obscure Inc.

3. **AGUILAR ELECTRONICS INC.** (USA) Electronic amplifiers 電子機器メーカー CD, AD: Stefan Sagmeister D: Veronica Oh DF: Sagmeister Inc.

4. **JUDITH CERVENKA** (USA) Welfare work 福祉 CD, AD, D: Evelyn Teploff

5. **MAN'S BEST PEN** (USA) Dog kennel manufacturer ドッグハウス メーカー D: Glenn Sweitzer DF: Fresh Design

6. **CLOTH DOLL ART** (USA) Doll manufacturer 人形メーカー AD, D: Janèl Apple DF: Kowalski Designworks, Inc.

1	2
3	4
5	6

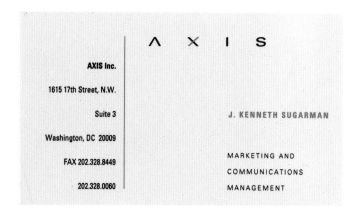

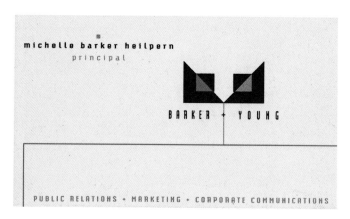

1. **AXIS, INC.** （USA） Marketing マーケティング AD, D: Samuel G. Shelton / Jeffrey S. Fabian D: Jean Kane DF: Kinetik Communication Graphics, Inc.

2. **ACCRAPLY INCORPORATED** （USA） Labeling equipment manufacturer ラベリング機器 メーカー CD, AD: John Reger D: Kobe DF: Design Center

3. **BARKER YOUNG** （USA） Marketing マーケティング CD, AD: Petrula Vrontikis D: Kim Sage DF: Vrontikis Design Office

4. **RIO NEVADA** （Canada） Mining 鉱業 AD, D: Catharine Bradbury DF: Bradbury Design Inc.

5. **FULL HOUSE CONTROL CORPORATION** （USA） Software ソフトウェア D: Nancy Skolos DF: Skolos / Wedell, Inc.

1 2
3
4 5

1. **LJUDMILA STRATIMIROVIĆ** (Yugoslavia) Hat manufacturer 帽子メーカー CD, AD, D: Škart DF: Škart Group

2. **MINISTRY OF CONSTRUCTION** (Japan) Government office 建設省
CD: Kenji Hanaue AD: D: Yoshiro Kajitani D: Michiko Arakawa CW: Hiroshi Hasegawa DF: Kajitani Design Room

1

2

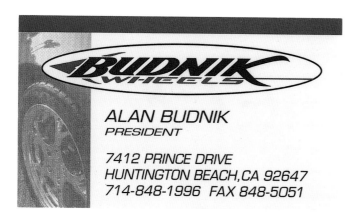

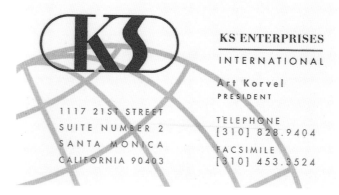

1. **BUDNIK WHEELS** （USA） Wheels manufacturer ホイール メーカー
CD, AD, D: Alan Middleton P: Randall Jachmann (Red Zone) DF: Middleton Performance Marketing

2. **KS ENTERPRISES** （USA） Trading company 貿易 CD, AD, D: Michael Chu DF: Mc design

3. **SBEMCO INTERNATIONAL** （USA） Carpet matting manufacturer カーペット メーカー CD, AD, D, I: John Sayles DF: Sayles Graphic Design

4. **CIRCLE MARKETING** （USA） Marketing マーケティング CD: Melanie Circle Brown AD, D: Eric Rickabaugh DF: Rickabaugh Graphics

5. **HAWAII THERMASTRUCTURES, INC.** （USA） Building systems ビル システム CD, AD, D, I, CW: Lani Isherwood DF: La Visage

6. **FERNANDO MACHUCA JR.** （USA） Steel fabrication スティール ファブリケーション CD, D: Fred Machuca DF: Machuca Design

1 2
3 4
5 6

Mêtier Furniture
Corporation

11200   215.
Roosevelt   673.
Boulevard   5300

Philadelphia,   Fax
Pennsylvania   676.
19115   7112

Donald Samuels, C.P.A.
Vice President, Finance

ELLEN MILIONIS

Manufacturing Services

85 Bergen Mills Road

Englishtown, NJ 07726

908/446-3120

(Fax) 908/792-0575

NEXTEC APPLICATIONS, INC.
PETER ELLMAN
PRESIDENT & CHIEF EXECUTIVE OFFICER
2717 LOKER AVE. WEST, CARLSBAD, CA 92008
PH 619 438 5533 X101 FX 619 438 5818

hightech ceram

Dr.-Ing. Detlef Steinmann

hightech ceram
Dr. Steinmann + Partner
GmbH

Rainerstraße 4
D-5358 Bad Münstereifel
Telefon 02253-8918
Telefax 02253-8256

Geschäftsführender Gesellschafter
Managing Partner

Peter Alge

Handel mit innovativer Friseurtechnik
Stiglingen 10, A-6850 Dornbirn
Telefon 0663/050669, Fax 05572/21261

1. **MÉTIER FURNITURE CORPORATION** （USA）Furniture manufacturer 家具メーカー D: Kerry Polite DF: Polite Design

2. **ELLEN MILIONIS** （USA）Book manufacturer ブック メーカー CD, AD, D, I: Jack Tom DF: Jack Tom Design

3. **NEXTEC APPLICATIONS, INC.** （USA）Fabric coating technology ファブリック コーティング
CD, AD, D: John Ball D: Kathy Carpentier-Moore .P: Various Stock Photographers DF: Mires Design, Inc.

4. **HIGHTECH CERAM** （Germany）Ceramics supplier セラミック CD, D: Detlef Behr DF: Detlef Behr, Büro für Kommunikationsdesign

5. **PETER ALGE** （Austria）Trading company 貿易 CD, AD, D: Sigi Ramoser

1 2
3
4 5

President
Norikazu Matsuo

Se Créer Inc. ◆ Mido Elphan Bldg.
4-3-12 Bakuro-machi Chuo-ku Osaka
541 Japan tel. 06-243-4168

EAST PERTH REDEVELOPMENT AUTHORITY

6TH FLOOR 19 PIER STREET

PERTH WESTERN AUSTRALIA 6000

FACSIMILE (09) 325 5016

TELEPHONE (09) 222 8000

Howard L. Morgan
President

1800 Walt Whitman Road
Melville, New York 11747
Tel: 516-752-3568
Fax: 516-752-3507

HUMANCAD™

A DIVISION OF BIOMECHANICS CORPORATION OF AMERICA

WENDELL B. SMITH, III

ORCHIDSOFT
P.O. BOX 3189 • 27420 ALPEN DRIVE • BLUE JAY, CA • 92317
(909) 337 - 0401 • FAX (909) 336 - 6046

Antonio Yung
Director

SOUTH HILL HOLDINGS LIMITED
CORPORATE OFFICE:
605 Cheung Lee Commercial Bldg.,
25 Kimberley Road, Kowloon, Hong Kong
Tel: 852 2732-2831 Fax: 852 2724-3884
U S A OFFICE:
7485 Rush River Way, #710-288
Sacramento, CA 95831 USA
Tel: 1 916-422-1123

江川　光宏

YOHJI YAMAMOTO ＋ NOIR

株式会社ヨウジデザイン研究所
〒140 東京都品川区東品川2-2-43-T33
Phone03-5463-1530 Fax.03-5463-1539

1. **SE CRÉER INC.** （Japan）Apparel maker **アパレル メーカー** AD, D: Sumihiro Takeuchi DF: Sumihiro Takeuchi Design Office
2. **EAST PERCH REDEVELOPMENT AUTHORITY** （Australia）Land development **土地開発** CD, AD, D, DF: Cato Design Inc.
3. **HUMANCAD** （USA）Software **ソフトウェア** CD, AD, D: Greg Walters DF: Greg Walters Design
4. **ORCHIDSOFT** （USA）Software **ソフトウェア** CD, AD: Stan Evenson D: Sheri Lambie DF: Evenson Design Group
5. **SOUTH HILL HOLDINGS LIMITED** （Japan）Self service photo equipment **ブースカメラ開発** D: Douglas Doolittle DF: Douglas Design Inc.
6. **YOHJI YAMAMOTO INC.** （Japan）Apparel maker **アパレル メーカー** CD, AD: Katsu Asano D: Kinue Yonezawa DF: ASA 100 Company

1 2
3 4
5 6

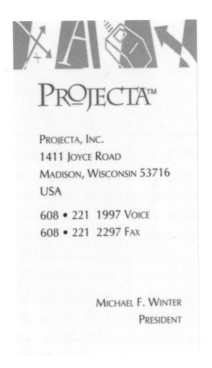

1. **ESQUISSE CO., LTD.** (Japan) Dressmaking patterns 服飾パターン メーカー AD, D: Sumihiro Takeuchi DF: Sumihiro Takeuchi Design Office

2. **HILLER WOHNBAU GMBH** (Austria) House-building ハウス メーカー CD, AD, D: Uwe Steinmayer

3. **ACCENTS ACCENT HARDWARE** (USA) Plumbing accessories 配管 CD, AD, D, I: Roger Yu DF: Goodson + Yu Design

4. **FUNCTION LTD.** (Greece) Computer systems コンピューター システム CD, AD, D: Leonidas Kanellos DF: Leonidas Kanellos Design Group

5. **PROJECTA, INC.** (USA) Software development ソフトウェア開発 CD, AD, D: Becky Chapman-Winter DF: Chapman-Winter Design

6. **PEGASUS MARKETING SERVICE, LIMITED** (Taiwan) Marketing マーケティング CD, AD, D: Chan Wing Kei, Leslie DF: Leslie Chan Design Co., Ltd.

1 2 3
4 5 6

tv
à la Carte

tv tv tv à la Carte à la Carte

tv
à la Carte

Willem de Zwijgerlaan 350
1055 RD Amsterdam

Postbus 56011
1040 AA Amsterdam

Telefoon: 020-584 88 88
Telefax: 020-400 30 25
Doorkiesnummer: 020-584 88 :

tv
à la Carte

Philip Roosegaarde Bisschop
Algemeen Directeur

tv
à la Carte

1. **KTA AMSTERDAM** （Netherlands） TV station テレビ局 CD: Ron Van Der Vlugt CD, D: Rob Verhaart DF: Designers Company

1

1. **KENIX CM**　(Japan)　TV advertising production　CM企画制作　D: Momoko Arakawa　DF: Super Kenix Inc.
2. **JONKERS HOFSTEE FILM**　(Netherlands)　Film company　映画会社　CD, D: Ron Van Der Vlugt　DF: Designers Company

URBANDALE INC.
TRAP & SKEET

RONALD J. ZAKRAJSEK

216) 298 3200
800) 896 5824

6347 LOVELAND ROAD
POST OFFICE BOX 333
MADISON, OHIO 44057

Greg Pope
Coordinator

Captain Planet Foundation

One CNN Center
Atlanta GA 30303

Phone 404 827 5368

Fax 404 827 4292

Internet: greg.pope@turner.com

Rick Rabuck
CREATIVE SERVICES

3221 HUTCHINSON AVE.
SUITE H
LOS ANGELES
CALIFORNIA 90034

Corporate Office 310 839 9211
Production Office 310 287 1228
Fax 310 815 0770

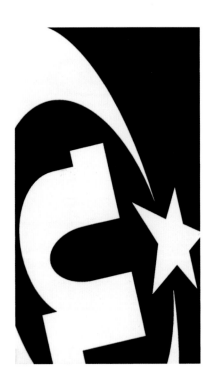

Printed with vegetable based inks on 100% recycled paper

1. **URBANDALE, INC.** (USA) Skeet shooting club 射撃場 CD, D: Molly J. Zakrajsek AD: Patty J. Palazzo DF: Triple Seven Design

2. **CAPTAIN PLANET FOUNDATION** (USA) TV cartoons アニメーション CD, D: Bjorn Akselsen AD: Pattie Belle Hastings DF: Icehouse Design

3. **GRAVITY FILMS** (USA) Film production 映像制作 CD: Rick Rabuck AD, D: Brian Burchfield
Fashion: David D'Angelo Product: Amedeo DF: Rabuck / Carnie Advertising, Inc.

1
2
3

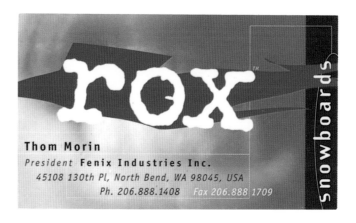

1. **SBK PICTURES INC.** （USA）Film and video production 映像、ビデオ D: Kerry Polite DF: Polite Design

2. **FENIX INDUSTRIES, INC.** （USA）Snowboards スノーボード CD, D: Daniel R. Smith P: Sean Bolan DF: Command Z

3. **FENIX INDUSTRIES, INC.** （USA）Snowboards スノーボード CD, D: Daniel R. Smith P: Sean Bolan DF: Command Z

HENRY FLOOD ROBERT, JR. · DIRECTOR

4160 BOULEVARD CENTER DRIVE · JACKSONVILLE, FLORIDA 32207

BUSINESS: (904)-398-8336 · FAX: (904)-348-3167

HOME: (904)-273-3011 · FAX: (904)-273-6566

JACKSONVILLE ART MUSEUM

CHALLENGES

Pink Noise SoundEnvironments™

HELLO.

PINK NOISE
305 East 46th Street, New York City, New York 10017-3058
Telephone: 212 371 1333 / Facsimile: 212 755 1737

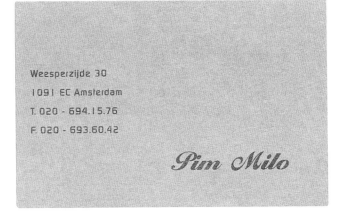

Weesperzijde 30
1091 EC Amsterdam
T. 020 - 694.15.76
F. 020 - 693.60.42

Pim Milo

'by Schwirtz/Milo/Meitner'

OPPOSITE PAGE: **PIERWSZY FILM / FIRST FILM** （Poland) Film production 映像制作 CD, AD, D, CW: Tadeusz Piechura DF: Atelier Tadeusz Piechura

1. **JACKSONVILLE ART MUSEUM** （USA) Art museum 美術館 CD, AD, D, I, CW: Jefferson Rall CD: Robin Shepherd DF: Robin Shepherd Studios

2. **PINK NOISE** （USA) Music studio 音楽スタジオ CD, AD: Stefan Sagmeister D, I: Eric Zim DF: Sagmeister Inc.

3. **BIG SHOTS GALLERY** （Netherlands) Photo gallery フォトギャラリー
CD, AD: Jacques Koeweiden / Paul Postma D: Eric Hesen P: Yani DF: Koeweiden Postma Associates

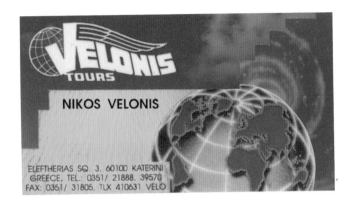

1. **VELONIS TOURS** (Greece) Travel agency 旅行会社 CD, D, CW: Apostolos Rizos AD, I: Tasos Efremidis DF: Alternation

2. **JAKES ATTIC** (USA) TV show ＴＶショー CD, AD, D: Sonia Greteman DF: Greteman Group

3. **EAR TO EAR** (USA) Music production 音楽制作 CD, AD, D: Scott Mires I: Tracy Sabin DF: Mires Design, Inc.

4. **FREIZEITZENTRUM WILLISAU** (Switzerland) Sports center スポーツセンター CD, AD, D, I, CW: Niklaus Troxler DF: Niklaus Troxler Design Studio, Willisau

5. **DREAMERS MUSIC CLUB** (Greece) Music club クラブ CD, AD, D: Leonidas Kanellos DF: Leonidas Kanellos Design Group

6. **FLATT** (Japan) Night club クラブ CD, AD, D: Sachi Sawada DF: Moss Design Unit

```
1 2
3 4
5 6
```

1. **SOUND INVESTMENTS** （USA）Pop memorabilia ポップ メモラビリア CD, AD, D: Ellie Leacock DF: Art Stuff

2. **MUSTANG RECORD** （Japan）Music production 音楽制作 CD, AD: Takazo Imai D: Tomio Shinohara I: Hirotaka Okamoto DF: Voice Corporation

3. **BERKMANN & GEIGER REISEN** （Austria）Travel agency 旅行会社 CD, AD, D, I: Sigi Ramoser

4. **JAM TAP DANCE COMPANY** （Japan）Tap dance タップダンス CD, AD, D: Mitsuhiro Hasegawa / Takehiko Ogane

5. **TERMINAL** （Greece）Night club クラブ CD, I, CW: Apostolos Rizos AD, D: Tasos Efremidis DF: Alternation

1 2
3 4
5

HENRIQUE OLIVIER MOREIRA

2 DE SETEMBRO, 325

BLUMENAU - SC

CEP. 89052-000

TEL./FAX:(0473)23 4727

BASE FRANQUEADORA DE VESTUÁRIO LTDA.

Muzeum Artystów ▲ The Artists' Museum

Tylna 14 ▲ 90-324 Łódź ▲ Poland ▲ tel./fax 042·741257

Jerzy Grzegorski

1. **BASE & CO.** （Brazil） Sportswear スポーツ用品 CD, D: Silvio Silva Junior CD: Mirian Hatori

2. **MUZEUM ARTYSTÓW** （Poland） Art museum 美術館 CD, AD, D: Tadeusz Piechura CW: Ryszard Waśko DF: Atelier Tadeusz Piechura

3. **SOL INC.** （Japan） Music production 音楽制作 AD: Kenji Koga

4. **HALSTED COMMUNICATIONS INC.** （USA） Communications コミュニケーション CD, AD: Petrula Vrontikis D: Kim Sage DF: Vrontikis Design Office

1 2
3
4

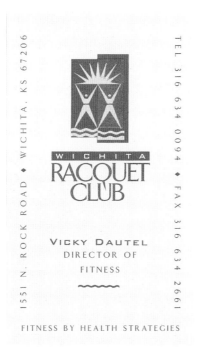

1. **WICHITA RACQUET CLUB** (USA) Fitness club フィットネス CD, AD, D: Sonia Greteman D: James Strange DF: Greteman Group

2. **RETRETTI** (Finland) Arts center アートセンター D: Viktor Kaltala DF: Viktorno Design Oy

3. **MAIN LINE HEALTH & FITNESS** (USA)、Fitness club フィットネス CD: Frederick Shamlian D, I: Steven Bagi D: Fred Shamlian DF: Shamlian Advertising

4. **PRIVATE EXERCISE** (USA) Fitness club フィットネス CD, AD: Stan Evenson D: Ken Loh DF: Evenson Design Group

5. **DIMITRA-REISEN** (Germany) Travel agency 旅行会社 CD, AD, D, I: Claudia Ochsenbauer

6. **NOVA TRAVEL** (USA) Travel agency 旅行会社 CD, AD, D: Sonia Greteman DF: Greteman Group

Dr. Elke Ludemann

Sportwissenschaften

Trainingslehre

Bewegungslehre

Kaiser-Karl-Ring 38 c

5300 Bonn 1

Telefon 0228-68 00 21

Telefax 0228-68 00 62

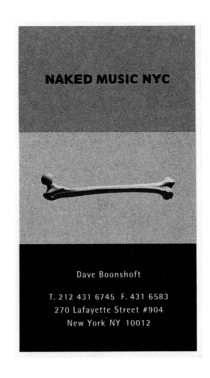

OPPOSITE PAGE: **XXX** （USA） Snowboards スノーボード CD, AD, D: Carlos Segura I: Tony Klassen DF: Segura Inc.

1. **COLOSSEUM** （Japan） Music events 音楽事業 CD: Noriyuki Ota AD: Hirosuke Ueno

2. **DR. ELKE LUDEMANN** （Germany） Sports science スポーツ科学 CD, D: Detlef Behr DF: Detlef Behr, Büro für Kommunikationsdesign

3. **NAKED MUSIC NYC** （USA） Music production 音楽制作 CD, AD: Stefan Sagmeister D: Veronica Oh P: Tom Schierlitz DF: Sagmeister Inc.

4. **HOTPIX** （USA） Music promotion 音楽プロモーション CD, AD, D: Ellie Leacock DF: Art Stuff

5. **KAS-KALÚ ACTIVE SYSTEM** （Brazil） Sportswear スポーツ用品 CD, D: Silvio Silva Junior CD: Mirian Hatori

6. **EXERCISE** （Greece） Fitness club フィットネス CD, AD, D: Leonidas Kanellos DF: Leonidas Kanellos Design Group

GENTLEMEN'S LOFT
SALON FOR MEN

Karen Barrett
609.429.3860

12 S. Haddon Avenue
Haddonfield, NJ 08033
Hours by appointment Mon thru Fri

JAPAN
JAZZ
AUDIENCE
ASSOCIATION

三澤隆宏

代表

ジャパン・ジャズ・オーディエンス・アソシエイション

川崎市麻生区王禅寺2729 〒215
TEL・FAX 044-951-3204

PSC

プロダクション・デスク
前田麻子

株式会社 PSC
〒107 東京都港区南青山 5-9-12 達沢ビル502 Tel: 03-3409-7294 Fax: 03-3409-1649

CHAMPION
PICTURES

Lindy Tamir

Champion Pictures Pty. Ltd.
Suite 9
437 St Kilda Road
Melbourne 3004
Australia
Phone (03) 9820 4688
Fax (03) 9820 4708

Palafox Communications, Inc.

368 Beverly Road · Douglaston, NY 11363
718 229-6373 fax 718 428-4731

MAUREEN LEGG
DIRECTOR OF
COMMUNICATIONS

CALIFORNIA
CENTER FOR
THE ARTS
ESCONDIDO

340 NORTH
ESCONDIDO BLVD

ESCONDIDO
CALIFORNIA
92025

PH 619 738 4138
FX 619 739 0205

OPPOSITE PAGE: **SHORT TERM MEMORY** (USA) Rock band ロックバンド CD, D, I: Cher Skoubo P: Peter M. Fredin DF: Skoubo Graphics
1. **GENTLEMEN'S LOFT** (USA) Executive men's salon メンズ サロン CD, AD, D, I: Wicky W. Lee DF: Wicky's Graphics
2. **JAPAN JAZZ AUDIENCE ASSOCIATION** (Japan) Jazz enthusiasts' group ジャズリスナー協会 AD, D: Fukushi Okubo DF: Fukushi Okubo Design Office
3. **PRODUCERS SYSTEM COMPANY INC.** (Japan) Film production 映画制作
AD: Mitsunobu Hosoyamada D, I: Hidehiro Yonekura I: Akiko Hamanaka DF: Hosoyamada Design Office
4. **CHAMPION PICTURES** (Australia) Film distribution 映画配給 AD, D: Andrew Hoyne D: Amanda McPherson DF: Andrew Hoyne Design
5. **PALAFOX COMMUNICATIONS** (USA) Video company ビデオ会社 CD, D: Melinda Beck DF: Melinda Beck Studio
6. **CALIFORNIA CENTER FOR THE ARTS** (USA) Arts center アート センター CD, AD, D: John Ball D: Miguel Perez DF: Mires Design, Inc.

1 2
3 4
5 6

Short Term Memory

81658
970.476.8919
970.476.2093

P.O. BOX 6278
VAIL, CO 81658
970.476.8919
970.476.2093
SM

Short Term Memory
Chet

6278
81658
476.8919
476.2093

SM

Short Term Memory
Lance Smith

short
term
memory

short
Term
Memory

Bradford
Segee

SM

P.O. BOX 6278
VAIL, CO 81658
970.476.8919
970.476.2093
SM

short
Term
Memory
Chet

SM

BOX 6278
CO 81658
476.8919
476.2093

P.O. BOX 6278
VAIL, CO 81658
970.476.8919
970.476.2093

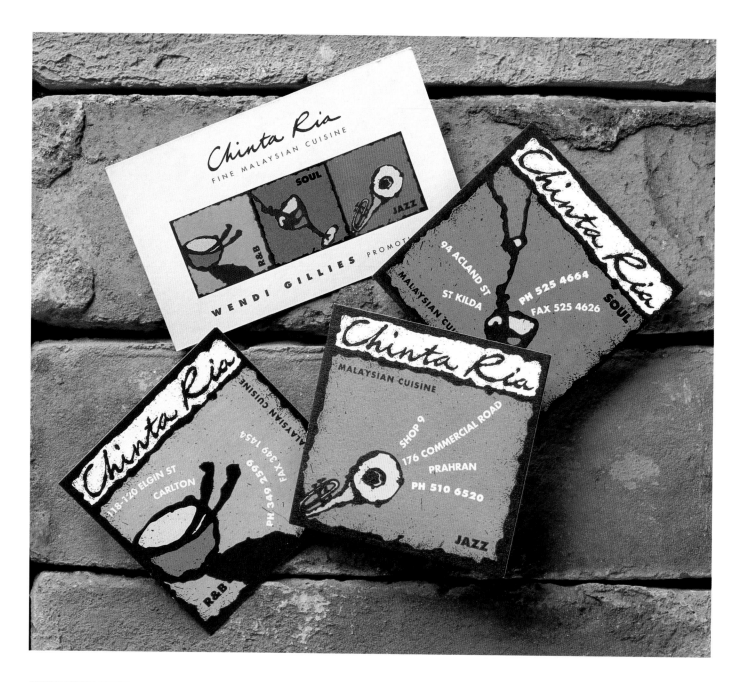

1. **CHINTA RIA** （Australia） Restaurant レストラン AD, D: Andrew Hoyne D, I: Simone Elder DF: Andrew Hoyne Design
2. **CHINTA RIA** （Australia） Restaurant レストラン AD, D: Andrew Hoyne I: Simone Elder DF: Andrew Hoyne Design
3. **B. STERN** （USA） Streetwear ストリート ウェア CD, AD, D: Evelyn Teploff I: Karl Wagoner
4. **STUSSY NEW YORK STORE** （USA） Apparel アパレル CD, AD, D: Shawn Stussy

古谷高治
furutani takaharu

タンクギャラリー
大阪市中央区西心斎橋2-10-12（GALLAGE内）phone : 06.211.4522 facsimile : 06.212.6532

SET FOR OUTDOOR ADVENTURE

鶴巻　昇

スーパージー
〒231 横浜市中区曙町4-56
Phone.045-231-0561

TEL.03-3862-1250 FAX.03-3862-1250
1-9-10 ASAKUSA-BASHI.TAITO-KU.TOKYO 111

有限
会社
サプライズ・
ザ・
プライス
surprise
the
price
company,
limited

....
マネージャー
manager

引地 智仁
tomohito hikichi

VINTAGE & FINECLOTHING
03-3791-7757

TANIGUCHI MITSUYASU

chusei bldg 2f,1-8-22,
higashi-shinsaibashi,chuo-ku,osaka,japan.
phone:06.243.0266

Takeshi Kawai

&mix
CLOSET

AND'S CLOSET MIX
1-8-22,Higashishinsaibashi,chuo-ku,osaka,JAPAN.
phone:06.244.4443 facsimile:06.282.1494

1. **TANK GALLERY** （Japan）Gallery cafe **カフェ** CD, AD, D: Sachi Sawada DF: Moss Design Unit

2. **SUPER G** （Japan）Outdoor goods **アウトドア ショップ** D: Yukiko Urushibara DF: Básis Inc.

3. **SURPRISE THE PRICE CO., LTD.** （Japan）Mail order **通信販売** AD, D: Takeshi Maeda

4. **FAB FOUR** （Japan）Household goods **雑貨店** CD: Tetsuyuki Takakuwa AD, D: Hideyuki Yoshida DF: Théas Co., Ltd.

5. **DIGA DIGA DOO** （Japan）Apparel **アパレル** CD, AD, D: Sachi Sawada DF: Moss Design Unit

6. **AND'S CLOSET MIX** （Japan）Apparel **アパレル** CD, AD, D: Sachi Sawada DF: Moss Design Unit

1　2
3　4
5　6

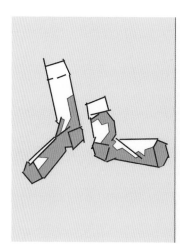

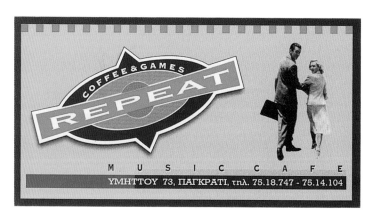

OPPOSITE PAGE: **STRANGE PARADISE** （Japan）Boutique　ブティック　AD, D: Katz-Miyake　DF: Miyake Design Office, Inc.

1. **CHAMPION** （Japan）Meat shop　**精肉店**　AD, D: Isamu Nakazawa　DF: Hi Hat Studio

2. **SLAP SHOT** （Japan）Apparel　アパレル　D: Slap Shot

3. **FASHION BOX JAPAN** （Japan）Apparel　アパレル　AD, D: Akira Utsumi

4. **THE STORE** （Netherlands）Boutique　ブティック　D: Robert van Rixtel / Goof Rutten　DF: PLAZA ontwerpers

5. **MURASAKI SPORTS** （Japan）Sports goods　スポーツ用品店　D: Murasaki Sports

6. **REPEAT** （Greece）Coffee shop　コーヒー専門店　CD, AD, D: Leonidas Kanellos　DF: Leonidas Kanellos Design Group

Our task is to create
a worthwhile encounter between
people and things; providing
people with something they
really wish to have.
We endeavor to search for
our customers' needs with
our expertise and creativity.
We are aiming to present
to you a shop where you
will always find yourselves
welcome and where, we
hope, you will find the items
you really want to have.

worthwhile encounter

SIX

小林弘道
Hiromichi
Kobayashi

**Manhattan
Records**

〒150 東京都渋谷区宇田川町10-1
Phone Number, 03-3477-7166.
Facsimile Number, 03-3477-0556.

私たちの仕事は、人と物との実りある
出会いを創造すること、つまり
「欲しいを売る」行為だと考えています。
どんな商品を、どういうお店に、
どのような態度で、そしてどんな方法で
売られていれば、「欲しい」という
情熱を持ってもらえるのか。お客様の
気持ちに、さらに私たちならこうである、
というわがままを添えて、sixはいつまでも
愛される新しい老舗を目指します。

シックス
152東京都目黒区
自由ヶ丘2-8-13
tel and fax
03 3723 7767

Tomomichi Shimizu

10-1, Udagawa-cho, Shibuya-ku,
ToKyo, Zip150, Japan.
Phone Number, 03-3477-7166.
Facsimile Number, 03-3477-0556.

1. **SIX** （Japan）Stationery store ステーショナリー ショップ AD, CW: Tatsuro Sato D: Hidetoshi Mito CW: Ikuko Hiroe

2. **SATELITES ART PLANNING INC.** （Japan）Fine art dealer 美術商 AD, D: Yoshihiro Madachi DF: Design Studio Waters

3. **MANHATTAN RECORDS** （Japan）Record store レコード店 AD, D: Yoshihiro Madachi DF: Design Studio Waters

1
2
3

上田久美

1. **OBARA SHUBEITEN** （Japan） Rice and liquor store 酒米店 CD: Masaaki Okada D: Yuko Furuse DF: Okada Design Office
2. **YUSUI-TEI** （Japan） Tofu restaurant 豆腐料理店 CD: Masaaki Okada D: Yuko Furuse DF: Okada Design Office
3. **CAMEL GALLERY** （Japan） Carpets カーペット AD, D: Hiroshi Morishima DF: Time-space-art Inc.
4. **JEWELRY EN** （Japan） Gemstone dealer 宝石商 CD, AD, D: Junko Kitamura DF: Tomboy Pro
5. **TERRA HOUSE** （Japan） Cake shop ケーキ ショップ D: Akihiko Tsukamoto
6. **SIPHON-TEI** （Japan） Coffee shop コーヒー専門店 AD, D: Sumihiro Takeuchi DF: Sumihiro Takeuchi Design Office

1 2
3 4
5 6

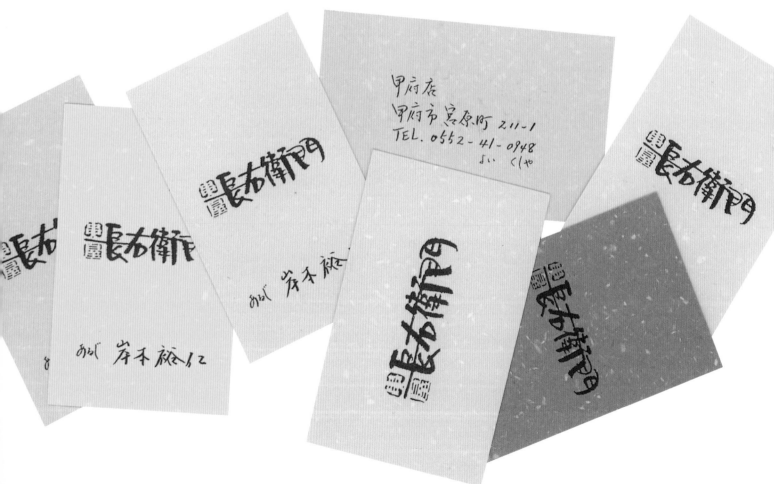

1. **SHATENKI** （Japan） Chinese restaurant 中華料理店 D, CW: Akira Takahashi DF: Básis Inc.

2. **DAIFUKU-YA** （Japan） Soba restaurant そば料理店 CD: Masaaki Okada AD: Yuko Furuse D: Kyoko Shoji DF: Okada Design Office

3. **GARLIC CHIPS INTERNATIONAL INC.** （Japan） Restaurant 飲食店 CD: Kansuke Yamamoto D: Hironobu Yamada

4. **CHOEMON** （Japan） Restaurant 飲食店 CD: Takayasu Muraoka D: Toru Akiyama DF: Akiyama & Co.

1 2 3

4

1. **JORDAN PUB** （Japan） Pub バブ CD, AD, D: Junko Kitamura DF: Tomboy Pro

2. **NANCY** （Japan） Fortune telling 占い CD, AD, D: Taketo Miyamoto

1

2

ERNESTO VILLELA NETO

AV. BATEL, 1546
TEL.: (041) 243 0515
FAX: (041) 225 4986
CURITIBA-PR
CEP. 80420-090

GUffO
BAR & RESTAURANTE

P.O. Box 1725 • Lihue, HI 96766 • 245-9593 • FAX: 246-1087

FOTÓGRAFO DE GENTE

Rua Br. do Serro Azul 252 ap. 1103
CEP 80020-180 • Curitiba • PR
Tel.: (041) 232 6402

WANTON WELLS
Good Food & Good Booze

17762 Mitchell
Irvine, CA
92714-6067

Phone
714/553-0101
800/953-2953

Fax
714/553-0387

Sterling Art

PÇA SAMOEL SABATINE, 200

LOJA 111

TEL (011) 458 9700

S. BERNARDO DO CAMPO - SP

CEP 09750 - 530

FAX (011) 4589027

Felissimo!

1. **GUFFO** (Brazil) Restaurant レストラン CD, D: Silvio Silva Junior CD: Mirian Hatori

2. **GAYLORD'S** (USA) Restaurant レストラン CD, AD, D, I, CW: Lani Isherwood DF: La Visage

3. **SOSSELLA** (Brazil) Design store デザイン ストア CD, D: Silvio Silva Junior CD: Mirian Hatori

4. **GARLIC CHIPS INTERNATIONAL INC.** (Japan) Restaurant 飲食店 CD: Karısuke Yamamoto D: Hironobu Yamada

5. **STERLING ART** (USA) Artist supply shop 画材屋 CD, D, I: Fred Machuca DF: Machuca Design

6. **FELISSIMO!** (Brazil) Restaurant レストラン CD: Silvio Silva Junior CD: Mirian Hatori D: Karine Mitsue Kawamura

1 2
3 4
5 6

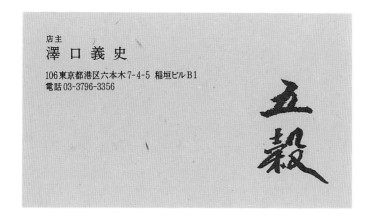

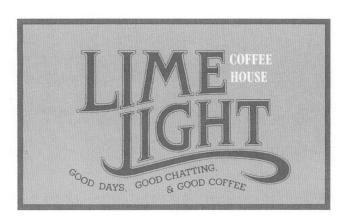

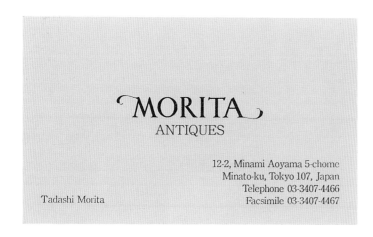

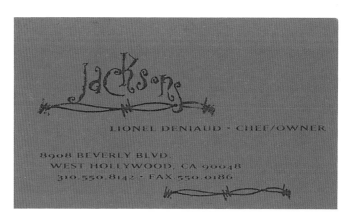

1. **GOKOKU** （Japan） Japanese restaurant 日本料理店 AD: Akihiko Tsukamoto D: Harumi Tominaga

2. **LIME LIGHT** （Japan） Coffee shop コーヒー専門店 AD, D: Sumihiro Takeuchi DF: Sumihiro Takeuchi Design Office

3. **HÔTEL DE MIKUNI** （Japan） French restaurant フランス料理店 D: Douglas Doolittle DF: Douglas Design Inc.

4. **MORITA ANTIQUES** （Japan） Antique shop 古美術品販売 D: Morita Antiques

5. **ALAN JACKSON** （USA） Restaurant レストラン CD, AD: Petrula Vrontikis D: Kim Sage DF: Vrontikis Design Office

GOLD KIOSK

SAMUEL GOLD 235 WEST 46 STREET NEW YORK 10036
RING 212 302 3819 **FAX** 212 354 5237

Danny First ©

270 N. Canon #1233
BeverLY-HiLLS CA. 90210
U.S.A TL: 213.464.49.11
FAX: 213.464.91.20

鞄/ORIGINAL & ORDER MADE

marzo

●マルゾ●
東京都渋谷区代々木4・40・1
ソフトタウン代々木110号　〒151
03・3372・1287(tel & fax)

Wok King

旺 WOK KING 正
Chinese Cuisine
318, I-95 Market
311 New Rodgers Road
Levittown PA 19056
(215)741-7155

IMPORT GOODS GALLERY
CRAZY DUCK
2-31-45 KITANAGASA-DORI CHUO-KU
KOBE JAPAN ZIP 650
TEL/FAX 078-333-7714

Evandro Portugal

raiz
QUADRADA
2

Rua Augusto Stresser, 183
Alto da Glória · Tel: (041) 253 4745
Fax: (041) 233 8841
Curitiba · Paraná · 80 030-340

OBJETOS DE DESIGN

1. **GOLD KIOSK** (USA) Design store デザイン ストア CD, AD, D: Nigel Walker DF: That's Nice
2. **DANNY FIRST** (USA) Boutique ブティック CD, AD, D: Danny First DF: Danny First Inc.
3. **MARZO** (Japan) Handbags バッグ店 AD: Hirosuke Ueno
4. **WOK KING CHINESE CUISINE** (USA) Chinese restaurant 中華料理店 CD, AD, D: Wicky W. Lee DF: Wicky's Graphics
5. **CRAZY DUCK** (Japan) Imported goods インポート グッズ CD, AD, D: Taketo Miyamoto DF: Miyamoto Design Office
6. **RAIZ QUADRADA (SQUARE ROOT)** (Brazil) Design store デザイン ストア CD, D: Silvio Silva Junior CD: Mirian Hatori

チーフデザイナー 野 瀬 牧 子
Makiko Nose

花港・HANA PORT
〒559 大阪市住之江区南港北1-14-16 大阪WTCB メールBox.No.218
TEL.06-615-6187 FAX.06-615-6188

代表取締役社長
戎 博司

株式会社 ニュー恵美須　長田店
〒653 神戸市長田区庄田町3-3-13
TEL 078-612-1603　FAX 078-611-3949
須磨パティオ店
〒654 神戸市須磨区中落合2-2-3
TEL 078-791-7220　FAX 078-791-3358

京都・錦本店／〒604 京都市中京区錦小路柳馬場西入 TEL.075-221-0088
阪急河原町店B1／阪急梅田店B1

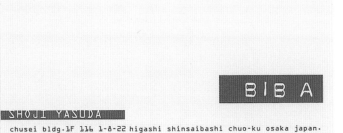

1. **MOTOR OIL JAPAN**（Japan）Apparel　アパレル AD, D: Akira Utsumi

2. **HANA PORT**（Japan）Flower shop　生花店　CD: Yoshihiko Watanabe　AD, D: Toru Date　DF: AI-D

3. **NEW EBISU**（Japan）Restaurant　レストラン　AD, D: Ciro Moritan

4. **KANEMATSU CO., LTD.**（Japan）Greengrocer　青果店　CD: Rie Terada　AD: Atsuko Satake　D: Rui Date　DF: Navvy Com

5. **BIB A**（Japan）Boutique　ブティック　CD, AD, D: Sachi Sawada　DF: Moss Design Unit

6. **HENRY**（Japan）Italian restaurant　イタリア料理店　CD, AD, D: Toru Date　DF: AI-D

1 2
3 4
5 6

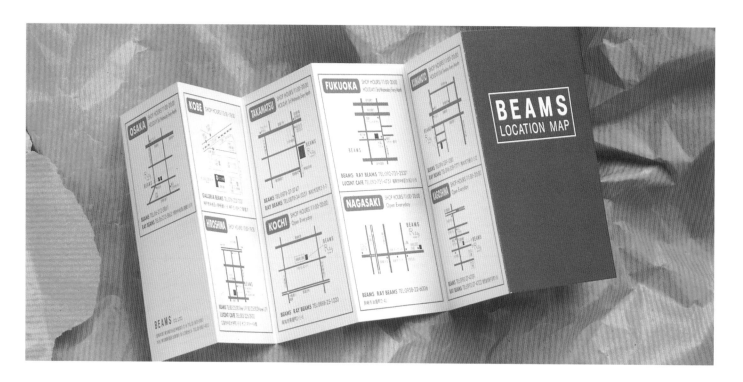

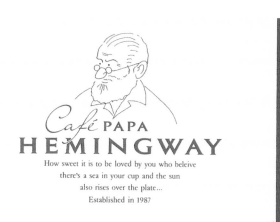

1. **BEAMS CO., LTD.** （Japan） Apparel アパレル CD: Yasushi Toritsuka D: Yukie Shibamata
2. **BON APPÉTIT** （Japan） Bar バー AD, D: Sumihiro Takeuchi DF: Sumihiro Takeuchi Design Office
3. **AND SO ON** （Japan） Boutique ブティック AD, D: Sumihiro Takeuchi DF: Sumihiro Takeuchi Design Office
4. **LE CHEF** （Brazil） French restaurant フランス料理店 CD, D: Silvio Silva Junior CD: Mirian Hatori
5. **CAFÉ PAPA HEMINGWAY** （Japan） Coffee shop コーヒー専門店 AD, D: Sumihiro Takeuchi DF: Sumihiro Takeuchi Design Office

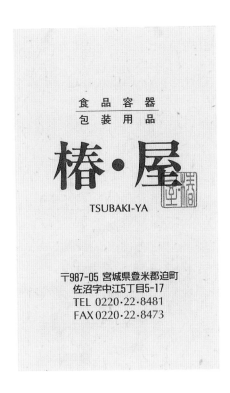

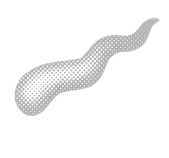

1. **TSUBAKI-YA** （Japan）Kitchen accessories 食品容器 CD: Masaaki Okada D: Yuko Furuse DF: Okada Design Office

2. **NAO** （Japan）Pub パブ CD, AD, D: Junko Kitamura DF: Tomboy Pro

3. **GARLIC CHIPS INTERNATIONAL INC.** （Japan）Restaurant 飲食店 CD: Kansuke Yamamoto D: Hironobu Yamada

4. **TABLE GALLERY INC.** （Japan）Chinaware 洋食器販売 D: Ruiko Urabe

5. **TAVOLINI** （Japan）Italian restaurant イタリア料理店 D: Douglas Doolittle DF: Douglas Design Inc.

1 2 3
4 5

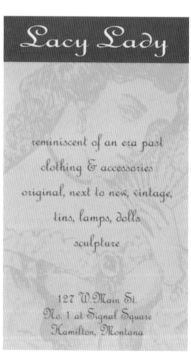

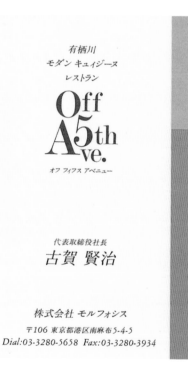

1. **BACCHUS** （Japan）Pub パブ CD, AD, D: Junko Kitamura DF: Tomboy Pro

2. **A-ONE INTERIOR** （USA）Interior boutique 家具店 CD, AD, D: Wicky W. Lee DF: Wicky's Graphics

3. **PIRETS BISTRO** （USA）Restaurant レストラン CD, AD, D: James Picquelle DF: Aloha Printing

4. **LACY LADY** （USA）Boutique ブティック AD, D: Janèl Apple DF: Kowalski Designworks, Inc.

5. **TEXTILE DIRECT SOURCE COMPANY** （China / Hong Kong）Textile shop テキスタイルショップ CD, AD, D, I: Wicky W. Lee DF: Wicky's Graphics

6. **MORPHOSIS INC.** （Japan）Restaurant レストラン AD: Kenji Koga

ALIMENTOS INFANTIS

Rua Oscar Gomes Cardim, 177
Tel.:(011)533 3096 • Fax(011)61 5287
São Paulo • SP • CEP 04 580-040

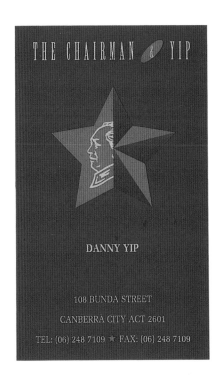

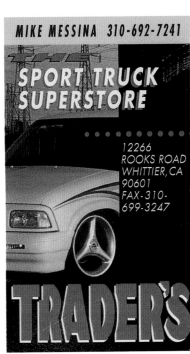

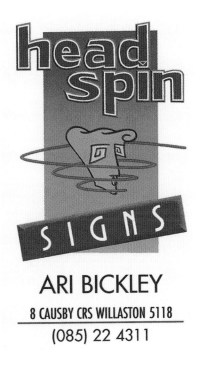

ARI BICKLEY

8 CAUSBY CRS WILLASTON 5118

(085) 22 4311

---

1. **STERLING ART** (USA) Artist supply shop 画材屋 CD, D, I: Fred Machuca DF: Machuca Design
2. **BICHO PAPÃO** (Brazil) Children's food 幼児用食品 CD, D: Silvio Silva Junior CD: Mirian Hatori
3. **THE CHAIRMAN & YIP** (Australia) Restaurant レストラン AD, D: Linda Fu DF: Linda Fu Design
4. **TRADER'S** (USA) Auto accessories オート アクセサリー
CD, AD, D, CW: Alan Middleton P: Randall Jackmann - Red Zone Photography DF: Middleton Performance Marketing
5. **HEAD SPIN** (Australia) Sign shop 看板 D, I: Ari Bickley P: Orange Lane Studios
6. **PICK UP** (Greece) Record shop レコード店 CD, D, CW: Apostolos Rizos AD, I: Tasos Efremidis DF: Alternation

1 2 3

4 5 6

1. **TIMBUKTUU COFFEE BAR** （USA） Restaurant レストラン CD, AD, D, I: John Sayles DF: Sayles Graphic Design

2. **801 STEAK & CHOP HOUSE** （USA） Restaurant レストラン CD, AD, D, I: John Sayles DF: Sayles Graphic Design

1. **BRAZIL RESTAURANT** （Germany） Restaurant レストラン CD, AD, D: Lilly Tomec

2. **MOCHA LISA** （USA） Bar and café バー CD, AD, D, I: Paula Bee DF: Paula Bee Design

3. **TEXTILIA** （USA） Design rugs デザイン ラグ CD, AD, D: Greg Walters DF: Greg Walters Design

1

2 3

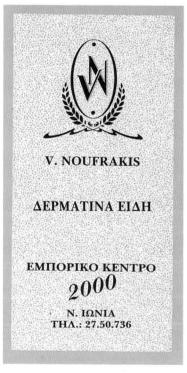

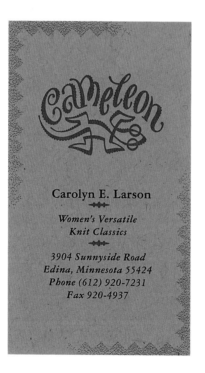

1. **CARDTERIA** （Japan） Greeting cards グリーティング カード CD: Frederick Shamlian D, I: Steven Bagi D, CW: Fred Shamlian DF: Shamlian Advertising

2. **IL NIDO** （Japan） Italian restaurant イタリア料理店 D: Douglas Doolittle DF: Douglas Design Inc.

3. **V. NOUFRAKIS** （Greece） Shoes 靴店 CD, AD, D: Leonidas Kanellos DF: Leonidas Kanellos Design Group

4. **CAMELEON** （USA） Boutique ブティック CD, AD: John Reger D: Sherwin Schwartzrock DF: Design Center

5. **HOSPITALITY RETAIL INC.** （USA） Hotel amenities ホテルアメニティ グッズ CD, AD, D: James Picquelle DF: Aloha Printing

1. **FULL MOON FOODS & MERCANTILE** （USA） Food market **食料品店** CD, AD, D: Mark Sackett D, I: Wayne Sakamoto DF: Sackett Design Associates

2. **PASSERELLE** （USA） Restaurant **レストラン** CD: Frederick Shamlian AD, D: Steven Bagi
D, CW: Fred Shamlian P: Barry Halkin I: Heidi Stevens / Susan Harvey DF: Shamlian Advertising

3. **GREEN ACRES** （USA） Food market **食料品店** CD, AD, D: Sonia Greteman DF: Greteman Group

4. **CAPONS ROTISSERIE CHICKEN** （USA） Restaurant **レストラン**
AD, D: Jack Anderson D, I: David Bates I: George Tanagi DF: Hornall Anderson Design Works, Inc.

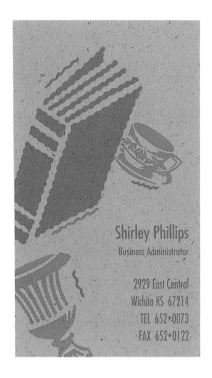

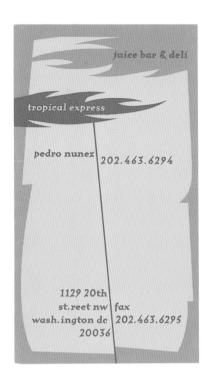

1. **GALLERIA FAIR** （USA） Retailer リテイラー CD, AD, D: Sonia Greteman DF: Greteman Group

2. **OAXACA GRILL** （USA） Restaurant レストラン CD, AD, D: Sonia Greteman D: Chris Parks DF: Greteman Group

3. **TROPICAL EXPRESS** （USA） Juice bar ジュース バー AD: Samuel G. Shelton / Jeffrey S. Fabian D: Mimi Massé DF: Kinetik Communication Graphics, Inc.

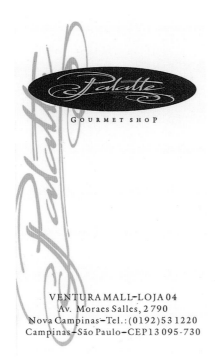

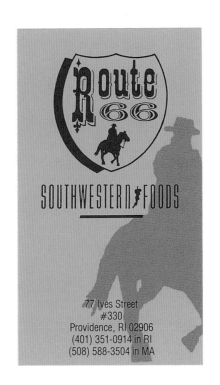

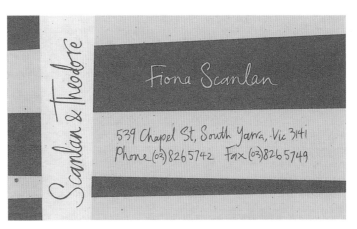

1. **PALLATE** (Brazil) Food market 食料品店 CD, D: Silvio Silva Junior CD: Mirian Hatori

2. **ROUTE 66 SOUTHWESTERN FOODS** (USA) Food market 食料品店 CD, AD, D, I: Marcia Romanuck DF: The Design Company

3. **SCANLAN AND THEODORE** (Australia) Boutique ブティック AD: Andrew Hoyne D, DF: Andrew Hoyne Design

4. **AVONLEA** (USA) Flower shop 生花店 CD, AD: John Reger D: Sherwin Schwartzrock DF: Design Center

1 2
3
4

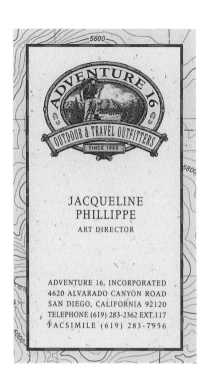

1. **LORENZO RISTORANTE ITALIANO** （Hong Kong） Italian restaurant イタリア料理店 CD: Kan Tai-keung
AD, D: Freeman Lau Siu Hong / Eddy Yu Chi Kong D: Benson Kwun Tin Yau I: Eddy Yu Chi Kong DF: Kan Tai-keung Design & Associates Ltd.

2. **ADVENTURE 16** （USA） Outdoor clothes アウトドア ショップ CD, AD, D: Jose Serrano I: Dan Thoner DF: Mires Design, Inc.

3. **KRATOCHWILL** （Slovenia） Pub パブ AD, D: Edi Berk DF: Krog, Ljubljana

4. **KOPF & SPIEGEL GMBH** （Austria） Work clothes 仕事着 CD, AD, D: Uwe Steinmayer

25 Fitzroy Street, St Kilda 3182 Telephone 525 4244

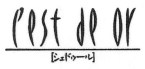

平田綾子
Ayako Hirata

〒530 大阪市北区曽根崎新地1-3-32　岡本センタービル2F
Phone 06(341)9977

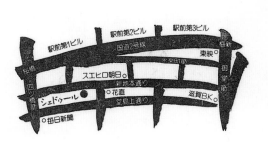

シェドゥール　曽根崎新地1-3-32 岡本センタービル2F　06(341)9977

1. **DINERS DE GALA** （Australia）Restaurant　レストラン　AD, D: Andrew Hoyne　DF: Andrew Hoyne Design

2. **LA VAISSELLE** （Japan）Chinaware　洋食品販売　CD: Kazuko Watanabe　AD: Akihiko Tsukamoto　D: Harumi Tominaga

3. **C'EST DE OR** （Japan）Bar　バー　CD, AD, D: Junko Kitamura　DF: Tomboy Pro

4. **GARLIC CHIPS INTERNATIONAL INC.** （Japan）Restaurant　飲食店　CD: Kansuke Yamamoto　D: Hironobu Yamada

5. **LIQUOR SHOP SHIGETA CO., LTD.** （Japan）Liquor shop　酒店　AD, D: Sumihiro Takeuchi　DF: Sumihiro Takeuchi Design Office

1. **CHICI MICKI** （Germany） Second hand clothes 古着 CD, AD, D: Uwe Steinmayer
2. **GIURLANI RISTORANTE ITALIANO** （Taiwan） Restaurant レストラン CD, AD, D: Chan Wing Kei, Leslie DF: Leslie Chan Design Co., Ltd.

1. **CRAWFORD DOYLE BOOKSELLERS** （USA） Book store 書店 CD, AD, D: Louise Fili I: Anthony Russo DF: Louise Fili Ltd.

2. **HASEGAWA ENTERPRISE LTD.** （Japan） Restaurant レストラン CD, AD: Petrula Vrontikis D: Kim Sage DF: Vrontikis Design Office

3. **HASEGAWA ENTERPRISE LTD.** （USA） Restaurant レストラン CD, AD: Petrula Vrontikis D: Lorna Stovall DF: Vrontikis Design Office

1

2 3

保田卓之

〒651
-21

自宅・神戸市西区玉津町水谷一二六一三
☎〇七八・九一一・七六八八

教室・明石市明南町二丁目一七一五
☎・Fax〇七八・九二八・九五〇九

〒673

Kagawaken Meizen Junior College
Kameoka-cho 1-10, Takamatsu
Kagawa 760 , JAPAN

TEL ; 81-878-33-3713
FAX; 81-878-37-1561

YOKO
MORITA

Gabi Schnell

Vordere Achmühle 24 b

A-6850 Dornbirn

Telefon 05 5 72 / 23 8 87

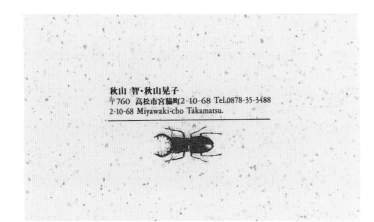

秋山　智・秋山晃子
〒760　高松市宮脇町2-10-68 Tel.0878-35-3488
2-10-68 Miyawaki-cho Takamatsu.

秋山　智・秋山晃子
〒760　高松市宮脇町2-10-68 Tel.0878-35-3488
2-10-68 Miyawaki-cho Takamatsu.

中村仁美

● 1928-27 Kita, Kawanishi-cho, Marugame. 0877-24-1912 ●

Hitomi NaKamura

● 1928-27 Kita, Kawanishi-cho, Marugame. 0877-24-1912 ●

Hitomi NaKamura

OPPOSITE PAGE: **TAKAYUKI YASUDA** （Japan） Personal use **個人用** CD: Masayuki Murakami D: Rie Morita I: Takayuki Yasuda DF: Creative Studio Bee Flight

1. **YOKO MORITA** （Japan） Personal use **個人用** D: Kaoru Miyazaki

2. **GABI SCHNELL** （Austria） Personal use **個人用** CD, AD, D, P: Sigi Ramoser

 TORU AKIYAMA （Japan） Personal use **個人用** D, I: Satoru Akiyama

 AMURA （Japan） Personal use **個人用** D: Satoru Akiyama

1 2
3
4

1. **CASA DE S. GABRIEL**（Portugal）Pedigree dogs ペット ショップ CD, AD, D: Emanuel Barbosa P: Rui Gaspar DF: Emanuel Barbosa Design

2. **VEREIN AKTION LEBEN VORARLBERG**（Austria）Social organization 社会団体 AD, D: Sigi Ramoser

3. **THE WARREN KNOWLES SOCIETY**（USA）Nature conservation 自然保護団体 CD, D: Jane Jenkins / Tom Jenkins DF: The Design Foundry

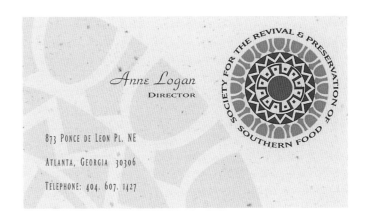

1. **GIORGIO ROMANO** (Switzerland) Medical services 医療 CD, AD, D: Oberholzer Tagli Knobel

2. **SOCIETY FOR THE REVIVAL & PRESERVATION OF SOUTHERN FOOD** (USA) Cultural organization 文化財団
CD, AD, D: Steve Rousso DF: Rousso + Associates

3. **SHIRAISHI / KAWADA** (Japan) Personal use 個人用 D: Satoru Akiyama

1 2

3

škart

000109

nisam
kriva

Mirjana
Bokšan

Beograd, decembar 1994.

000064

škart

Branko
Pavić

ima
zlatne ruke

u

zlatnom
oku

Novi Sad, 9. decembar 1994.

i samo je proleć'o sneg.

Danica P.
(krojačica
u penziji)

000085
kraj zime, Beograd 1995.

škart

OPPOSITE PAGE: **MIRJANA BOKŠAN / BRANKO PAVIĆ / DANICA P.** (Yugoslavia) Personal use 個人用 CD, AD, D, CW: Škart DF: Škart Group

1. **MARIUSZ WIECZOREK** (Poland) Personal use 個人用 CD, AD, D: Tadeusz Piechura CW: Mariusz Wieczorek DF: Atelier Tadeusz Piechura

2. **OLLI REIMA** (Poland) Personal use 個人用 CD, AD, D: Tadeusz Piechura CW: Olli Reima DF: Atelier Tadeusz Piechura

3. **FRAUKE + THOMAS** (Germany) Personal use 個人用 CD, D: Detlef Behr DF: Detlef Behr, Büro für Kommunikationsdesign

4. **GOODS FOR GUNS FOUNDATION INC.** (USA) Social organization 社会団体 CD, AD, D, I: Mike Quon CD: A. Morris DF: Mike Quon Design Office

5. **JAPAN RACE ORGANIZATION** (Japan) Racing organization レース協会 D: Douglas Doolittle DF: Douglas Design Inc.

6. **WYDZIAL KULTURY SPORTU I TURYSTYKI** (Poland) Department of culture 文化事業
CD, AD, D: Tadeusz Piechura CW: Lech W. Leszczynski DF: Atelier Tadeusz Piechura

```
1 2
3 4
5 6
```

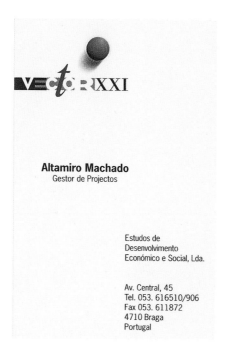

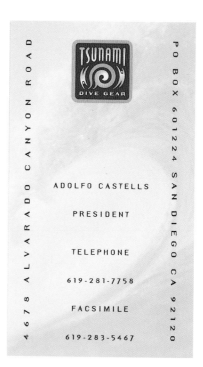

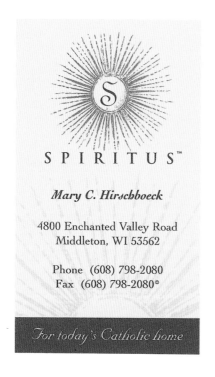

1. **PHIL BUECHLER MINISTRIES** (USA) Religious organization 宗教団体 CD, AD, D: John Reger DF: Design Center

2. **VECTOR XXI** (Portugal) Social organization 社会団体 CD, AD, D, I: Emanuel Barbosa DF: Emanuel Barbosa Design

3. **TSUNAMI** (USA) Diving gear ダイビング関連事業 CD, AD, D: John Ball DF: Mires Design, Inc.

4. **SPIRITUS** (USA) Religious goods 宗教関連事業 CD, D: Jane Jenkins / Tom Jenkins DF: The Design Foundry

5. **HITACHI, LTD. MAGICIANS CLUB** (Japan) Magic circle 奇術部 AD, D: Toshihiro Onimaru DF: Graphics & Designing Inc.

6. **KAREN BURNS** (USA) Personal use 個人用 D: Alison Scheel DF: The Design Company

P R E S T O N
B A P T I S T
C H U R C H

Gary Moen
Pastor

31104 S.E. 86th St.
Post Office Box 948
Preston, WA 98050
(206) 222-5573

GraphicDesigner (Macintosh Layout)

KAORU MIYAZAKI

internet adress: s93g519@ed.kagawa-u.ac.jp
home: 0878-26-3396 office: 0878-36-1666

日本大学芸術学部 映画学科

太田貴也

〒227 横浜市緑区田奈町12-46
TEL. 045(981)7048

President
渡辺義彦
Yoshihiko Watanabe

LOBBYIST
JAPAN

TELEPHONE **06.656.4115**
FACSIMILE **06.675.6979**

株式会社 ロビイスト・ジャパン

559 大阪市住之江区浜口西3-1-2-1101

1. **HONMOKU JINJA** (Japan) Shinto shrine 神社 CD: Toshio Koizumi AD, D: Murray Swift DF: Prime Corporation
2. **ARIANES** (France) Engineering 工学 CD, AD, D: Jean-Jacques Tachdjian
3. **PRESTON BAPTIST CHURCH** (USA) Church 教会 CD, AD, D: Rick Eiber DF: Rick Eiber Design
4. **KAORU MIYAZAKI** (Japan) Personal use 個人用 D: Kaoru Miyazaki
5. **TAKAYA OTA** (Japan) Personal use 個人用 CD, AD, D: Tetsuya Ota
6. **LOBBYIST JAPAN CO., LTD.** (Japan) Election services 選挙関連業務 CD: Yoshihiko Watanabe AD, D: Toru Date DF: AI-D

1 2 3
4 5 6

GreenStreet.

Gary Abbott

GreenStreet Company, Inc.
P.O. Box 1385 / 12810 178th Suite 105
Woodinville, WA 98072
Ph. (206) 486-3705 / Fax (206) 483-2541

GREENSTREET （USA） Product development 商品開発 CD: Gary Abbott AD, D: Michael Strassburger DF: Modern Dog

INDEX OF CONTRIBUTORS

INDEX OF CONTRIBUTORS

INDEX OF CONTRIBUTORS

New Business Card Graphics

Editorial Credits

Art director
Douglas Gordon

Designer
Fumie Takeuchi

Editor
Etsuko Kitagami

Photographer
Kuniharu Fujimoto

Coordinators
Chizuko Gilmore
Clive Avins

English translator & consultant
Sue Herbert

Publisher
Shingo Miyoshi

1996年 3月 28 日初版第 1 版発行

発行所　ピエ・ブックス
〒170 東京都豊島区駒込4-14-6-301
TEL: 03-3949-5010 FAX: 03-3949-5650

製版・印刷・製本　（株）サンニチ印刷
〒151 東京都渋谷区代々木2-10-8
ケイアイ新宿ビル
TEL: 03-3374-6242 FAX: 03-3374-6252

©1996 P·I·E BOOKS Printed in Japan
ISBN4-89444-004-0 C3070P16000E

BROCHURE & PAMPHLET COLLECTION Vol. 4
好評！業種別カタログ・コレクション、第4弾
Pages: 224 (Full Color) ￥16,000
The fourth volume in our popular "Brochure & Pamphlet" series. Twelve types of businesses are represented through artwork that really sells. This book conveys a sense of what's happening right now in the catalog design scene. A must for all creators.

BROCHURE DESIGN FORUM Vol. 2
世界の最新カタログ・コレクション
Pages: 224 (176 in Color) ￥16,000
A special edition of our "Brochure & Pamphlet Collection" featuring 250 choice pieces that represent 70 types of businesses and are classified by business for handy reference. A compendium of the design scene at a glance.

COMPANY BROCHURE COLLECTION
業種別（会社・学校・施設）案内グラフィックス
Pages: 224 (192 in Color) ￥16,000
A rare selection of brochures and catalogs ranging from admission manuals for colleges and universities, to amusement facility and hotel guidebooks, to corporate and organization profiles. The entries are classified by industry for easy reference.

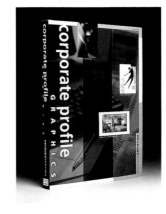

CORPORATE PROFILE GRAPHICS
世界の会社案内グラフィックス
Pages: 224 (Full Color) ￥16,000
A new version of our popular "Brochure and Pamphlet Collection" series featuring 200 carefully selected catalogs from around the world. A substantial variety of school brochures, company profiles and facility information are offered.

CREATIVE FLYER GRAPHICS
世界のチラシ・グラフィックス
Pages: 224 (176 in Color) ￥16,000
Features about 500 rigorously screened flyers and leaflets. Here, as nowhere else, you see what superior graphics can accomplish on a single sheet of paper. This is an invaluable reference that will become your behind-the-scenes partner in advertising production for years to come.

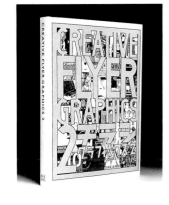

CREATIVE FLYER GRAPHICS Vol. 2
好評！世界のチラシ・グラフィックス、第2弾
Pages: 224 (Full Color) ￥16,000
A pack of some 600 flyers and leaflets incorporating information from a variety of events including exhibitions, movies, plays, concerts, live entertainment and club events, as well as foods, cosmetics, electrical merchandise and travel packages.

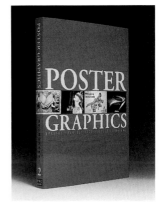

POSTER GRAPHICS Vol. 2
好評！業種別世界のポスター集大成、第2弾
Pages: 256 (192 in Color) ￥17,000
700 posters from the top illustrators in Japan and abroad are showcased in this book - classified by business. This invaluable reference makes it easy to compare design trends among various industries and corporations.

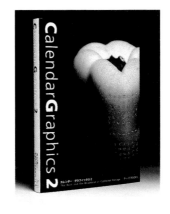

CALENDAR GRAPHICS Vol. 2
好評カレンダー・デザイン集の決定版、第2弾
Pages: 224 (192 in Color) ￥16,000
The second volume of our popular "Calendar Graphics" features designs from about 250 1994 and 1995 calendars from around the world. A rare collection including those on the market as well as exclusive corporate PR calendars.

BUSINESS PUBLICATION GRAPHICS
業種別ＰＲ誌の集大成！
Pages: 224 (Full Color) ￥16,000
This comprehensive graphic book introduces business publications created for a variety of business needs, including promotions from boutiques and department stores, exclusive clubs, local communities and company newsletters.

TRAVEL & LEISURE GRAPHICS
ホテル＆旅行 案内 グラフィックス
Pages: 224 (Full Color) ￥16,000
A giant collection of some 400 pamphlets, posters and direct mailings exclusively delivered for hotels, inns, resort tours and amusement facilities.

SPECIAL EVENT GRAPHICS
世界のイベント・グラフィックス
Pages: 224 (192 in Color) ￥16,000
A showcase for event graphics, introducing leaflets for exhibitions, parties, fashion shows, symposiums, all sorts of sales promotional campaigns, posters, premiums and actual installation scenes from events around the world. An invaluable and inspirational resource book, unique in the world of graphic publishing.

CORPORATE IMAGE DESIGN
世界の業種別ＣＩ・ロゴマーク
Pages: 336 (272 in Color) ￥16,000
An effective logo is the key to brand or company recognition. This sourcebook of total CI design introduces pieces created for a wide range of businesses - from boutiques to multinationals - and features hundreds of design concepts and applications.

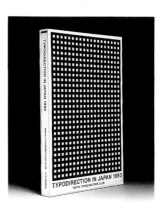

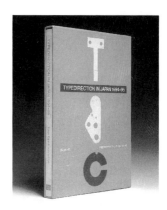

RETAIL IDENTITY GRAPHICS
世界のショップ・グラフィックス
Pages: 208 (176 in Color)　￥14,800
150 retail outlets from all over the world are featured for outstanding graphic design. This book is a choice collection of every kind of retail graphic from restaurant menus, business cards and signs to complete interior and exterior motifs.

DIAGRAM GRAPHICS Vol. 2
世界のダイアグラム・デザインの集大成
Pages: 224 (192 in Color)　￥16,000
The unsurpassed second volume in our "Diagram Graphics" series is now complete, thanks to cooperation from artists around the world. It features graphs, charts and maps created for various media.

TYPO-DIRECTION IN JAPAN Vol. 5
年鑑 日本のタイポディレクション '93
Pages: 254 (183 in Color)　￥17,000
A total of 600 award-winning typographic works from around the world are shown in this one book. It includes recent masterpieces by eminent art directors and designers as well as powerful works by up-and-coming designers. This is a book bound to fuel the current typography boom.

TYPO-DIRECTION IN JAPAN Vol. 6
年鑑 日本のタイポディレクション '94-'95
Pages: 250 (Full Color)　￥17,000
This book features the finest work from the international competition of graphic design in Japan. The sixth volume of our popular yearbook series is edited by the Tokyo Directors Club with the participation of master designers worldwide.

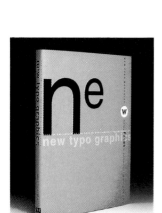

ALL OF SSAWS
ザウスのCI、アプリケーション＆グッズ
Pages: 120 (Full Color)　￥3,800
The graphics of SSAWS - the world's No. 1 all season ski dome is showcased in this publication; everything from CI and rental wear to signs. This is the CI concept of the future - design that changes, evolves and propagates freely through its own space. Don't miss this one.

NEW TYPO GRAPHICS
世界の最新タイポグラフィ・コレクション
Pages: 224 (192 in Color)　￥16,000
Uncompromising in its approach to typographic design, this collection includes 350 samples of only the very finest works available. This special collection is a compendium of all that is exciting along the leading edge of typographic creativity today.

1, 2 & 3 COLOR GRAPHICS
1・2・3色グラフィックス
Pages: 208 (Full Color)　￥16,000
Featured here are outstanding graphics in limited colors. See about 300 samples of 1,2 & 3-color artwork that are so expressive they often surpass the impact of full four-color reproductions. This is a very important book that will expand the possibilities of your design work in the future.

1, 2 & 3 COLOR GRAPHICS Vol. 2
1・2・3色グラフィックス、第2弾
Pages: 224 (Full Color)　￥16,000
Even more ambitious in scale than the first volume, this second collection of graphics displays the unique talents of graphics designers who work with limited colors. An essential reference guide to effective, low-cost designing.

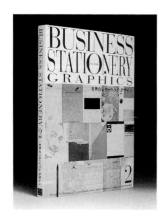

BUSINESS STATIONERY GRAPHICS
世界のレターヘッド・コレクション
Pages: 224 (192 in Color)　￥15,000
Long gone are the days when stationery meant a blank sheet of paper with a company name and address. The aim of this volume is to present all the components of today's most original corporate stationery systems.

BUSINESS STATIONERY GRAPHICS Vol. 2
世界のレターヘッド・コレクション、第2弾
Pages: 224 (176 in Color)　￥16,000
The second volume in our popular "Business Stationery Graphics" series. This publication focuses on letterheads, envelopes and business cards, all classified by business. Our collection will serve artists and business people well.

BUSINESS CARD GRAPHICS Vol. 1 / Soft Jacket
世界の名刺コレクション／ソフトカバー
Pages: 224 (160 in Color)　￥3,800
First impressions of an individual or company are often shaped by their business cards. The 1,200 corporate and personal-use business cards shown here illustrate the design strategies of 500 top Japanese, American and European designers. PIE's most popular book.

BUSINESS CARD GRAPHICS Vol. 2
世界の名刺＆ショップカード、第2弾
Pages: 224 (192 in Color)　￥16,000
Even bigger than the first edition! Outstanding business cards gathered from all over the world. Guaranteed not to let you down.

POSTCARD GRAPHICS Vol. 3
好評! 業種別ポストカードの第3弾
Pages: 232 (208 in Color)　¥16,000
Direct mail postcards can shock, intrigue or amuse, but they must always inform. This collection of 1,500 corporate and personal-use postcards from Japan and around the world features designs for companies, retailers and fashion houses.

POSTCARD GRAPHICS Vol. 4
世界の業種別ポストカード・コレクション
Pages: 224 (192 in Color)　¥16,000
Our popular "Postcard Graphics" series has been revamped for "Postcard Graphics Vol. 4." This first volume of the new version showcases approximately 1,000 pieces ranging from direct mailers to private greeting cards, selected from the best around the world.

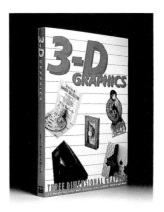

3-D GRAPHICS
3Dグラフィックスの大百科
Pages: 224 (192 in Color)　¥16,000
350 works that demonstrate some of the finest examples of 3-D graphic methods, including DMs, catalogs, posters, POPs and more. The volume is a virtual encyclopedia of 3-D graphics.

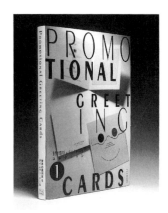

PROMOTIONAL GREETING CARDS ADVERTISING GREETING CARDS Vol. 4 (English Title)
世界の案内状＆ダイレクトメール集大成
Pages: 224 (Full Color)　¥16,000
A total of 500 examples of cards from designers around the world. A whole spectrum of stylish and inspirational cards, ranging from corporate invitations to private wedding announcements, are classified by function for easy reference.

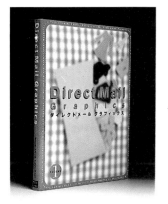

DIRECT MAIL GRAPHICS Vol. 1
衣・食・住のセールスDM特集
Pages: 224 (Full Color)　¥16,000
The long-awaited design collection featuring direct mailers with outstanding sales impact and quality design. 350 of the best pieces, classified into 100 business categories. A veritable textbook of current direct-marketing design.

DIRECT MAIL GRAPHICS Vol. 2
好評! 衣・食・住のセールスDM特集! 第2弾
Pages: 224 (Full Color)　¥16,000
The second volume in our extremely popular "Direct Mail Graphics" series features and classifies by industry a whole range of direct mailers for various purposes; from commercial announcements to seasonal greetings.

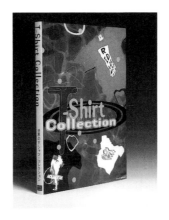

T-SHIRT GRAPHICS / Soft Jacket
世界のTシャツ・コレクション / ソフトカバー
Pages: 224 (192 in Color)　¥3,800
This stunning showcase publication features about 700 T-shirts collected from the major international design centers. Includes various promotional shirts and fabulous designs from the fashion world and sporting-goods manufacturers as well. This eagerly awaited publication has arrived at just the right time.

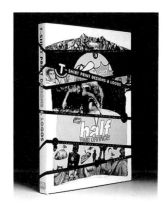

T-SHIRT PRINT DESIGNS & LOGOS
世界のTシャツ・プリント デザイン＆ロゴ
Pages: 224 (192 in Color)　¥16,000
Volume 2 of our popular "T-shirt Graphics" series. In this publication, 800 designs for T-shirt graphics, including many trademarks and logotypes are showcased. The world's top designers in the field are featured.

The Paris Collections / INVITATION CARDS
パリ・コレクションの招待状グラフィックス
Pages: 176 (Full Color)　¥13,800
This book features 400 announcements for and invitations to the Paris Collections, produced by the world's top names in fashion over the past 10 years. A treasure trove of ideas and pure fun to browse through.

FASHION & COSMETICS GRAPHICS
ファッション＆コスメティック・グラフィックス
Pages: 208 (Full Color)　¥16,000
We have published a collection of graphics from around the world produced for apparel, accessory and cosmetic brands at the vanguard of the fashion industry. A total of about 800 labels, tags, direct mailers, etc., from some 40 brands featured in this book point the way toward future trends in advertising.

SPORTS GRAPHICS / Soft Jacket
世界のスポーツグッズ・コレクション / ソフトカバー
Pages: 224 (192 in Color)　¥3,800
A collection of 1,000 bold sporting-goods graphic works from all over the world. A wide variety of goods are shown, including uniforms, bags, shoes and other gear. Covers all sorts of sports: basketball, skiing, surfing and many, many more.

LABELS AND TAGS COLLECTION Vol. 1 / Soft Jaket
ラベル＆タグ・コレクション / ソフトカバー
Pages: 224 (192 in Color)　¥3,800
Nowhere is brand recognition more important than in Japan. Here is a collection of 1,600 labels and tags from Japan's 450 top fashion names with page after page of women's and men's clothing and sportswear designs.

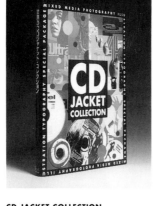

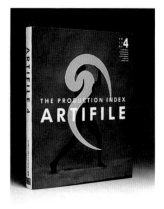
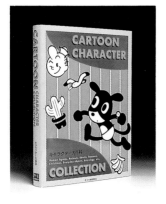